RAF BECCLES AT WAR, 1943-45

MALCOLM R. HOLMES

PRICE £4.95 NETT

Copyright : Malcolm R. Holmes

First published in the UK in 1994 by:

Malcolm R. Holmes
49, Meadow Gardens
Beccles
Suffolk NR34 9PA

Revised 2010

ISBN 978-0-9523443-2-2

Printed by

The Bidnall Press Limited
Unit 37
Ellough Industrial Estate
Beccles
Suffolk NR34 7TD

Cover design includes part of an original painting by Joe Crowfoot, titled 'Warwick at Ellough'

For further examples of Joe's work, log on to:
www.joecrowfootartist.co.uk

BIBLIOGRAPHY

Airfields and Airstrips, Part 1, by the Norfolk & Suffolk Aviation Society
Military Airfields in the British Isles, 1939-1945, by Steve Willis & Barry Hollis
Action Stations I, by Chaz Bowyer
Aeronauts and Aviators, by Christopher Elliott
The Mighty Eighth, by Roger A. Freeman
The Mighty Eighth War Diary, by Roger A. Freeman
Mighty Eighth War Manual, by Roger A. Freeman
B-17 Fortress at War, by Roger A. Freeman
Fields of Little America, by Martin Bowman
"My War" 1939-46, by Andy Padbury
Squadrons of the RAF, by Wing Commander Jefford
German & Allied Secret Weapons of the 2nd World War, by Ian Hogg & J.B.King
Mosquito - The Original Multi-Role Aircraft, by Graham M.Simmons
Bombs Gone, by Wing Commander J.A.MacBean & Major A.S.Hogben
Barnes Wallis, by J.E.Morpurgo
The Secret War, by Brian Johnson
Murder in East Anglia, by Robert Church
Flight over the Eastern Counties, by Gordon Kinsey
Vickers Aircraft since 1908, by C.F.Andrews
Fairey Aircraft since 1915
The Underwater War, 1939-45, by Richard Compton-Hall
Axis Submarines, by Anthony J.Watts
Sea Battles in Close Up, World War 2, Volume 2, by Eric Grove
Encyclopaedia of the Fleet Air Arm, by Paul Beaver
A Most Secret Squadron, by Des Curtis

CONTENTS

Acknowledgements

Introduction

1	Beginnings : The American Connection	1
2	Most Secret Squadron	13
3	The Rescuers	21
4	Murder in Green Lane	27
5	"We Shall be There"	32
6	"Like a Thunderbolt from Heaven"	44
7	Return to Peace	51
8	Endings and Beginnings	57

ACKNOWLEDGEMENTS

The preparation of this book has only been possible with the assistance of a wide variety of people and organisations. If any contributors have been missed from the following list, I apologise sincerely, and thank all who have provided information, photographs, recollections and support.

278 Sqn RAF - Phil Rounce, Jay Steen, Tim Coles
279 Sqn RAF - Gerald Austin
280 Sqn RAF - Gus Platts, Andy Padbury, Jim Forrest, Stan Gibbs Charles Goldspink, David Hasprey, Steve Dawson
618 Sqn RAF - Des Curtis, Leon Murray
810 Sqn FAA - Eric Waterson, James Moorhouse, Victor Leese, Derek Rhodes, Andrew Phillip, John Charlton
827 Sqn FAA - Nelson Abraham, K.W.Mapp
38th Bomb Group USAAF – Bob McWhite
401st Bomb Group USAAF – Dan Knight
Ground Staff - E.Hinchcliffe, Fred Root
Local Residents - L.M.Youngs, David Woodward, Nathan Warne, Christopher Elliott
Historians - Dick Wickham, Sid Harvey, John Archer, Bob Collis, Stephen Daniels, K.P. Bannerman, Ian McGlachlan
Associations - Aircrew Association, Fleet Air Arm Officer's Assn, Telegraphist Air Gunners Association
Miscellaneous - Flypast Magazine, Merlin Books Ltd, Staff of Beccles Town Library, RAF Museum, Imperial War Museum Photographic Dept, Fleet Air Arm Museum, Public Records Office, Norfolk and Suffolk Aviation Museum, British Aerospace, South Pickenham Estates Ltd, Phillip Jarrett, Joe West, Rainer and Marcia Forster, Bob Ward
Centre Pages - Crown Copyright/MoD. Reproduced with the permission of the Controller of HMSO.

With Special Thanks to:

JOE CROWFOOT, for capturing the spirit of this book with paintbrush

All proceeds from the sale of this book will be shared between Help for Heroes and the Gurkha Welfare Trust.

INTRODUCTION

My research into RAF Beccles began in 1990, initially as an exercise to try to uncover more about the airfield's wartime history, a resulting book being furthest from my mind. As I discovered more information and contacts, it became apparent that very little was known beyond the bare facts of unit and aircraft movements, as well as a neglect of a major element of the wartime activity there and at many other airfields round the country - Coastal Command's Air Sea Rescue organisation.

The airfield has always held a haunting fascination for me. With an early interest in all things aviation related, I was drawn to "Ellough Airfield", as I knew it, by anything from the scale models of the Waveney Model Flying Club on a Sunday afternoon to a frantic cycle ride from home to catch a glimpse of a crop spraying Pawnee or a Heron four engine executive transport gracing the runways. I often imagined Liberators and Fortresses lumbering from the hot tarmac on summer's day, drowning the chattering skylarks which were often the only thing airborne during the time I spent there. The illusion of an American base was born out by the tower design, scattered Nissen hut accommodation and two large black T2 hangars dominating the scene. It was no surprise to learn of it's intended use as a heavy bomber base for the 8th United States Army Air Force, and any disappointment I may have felt was replaced by the interest in discovering the RAF and Fleet Air Arm's association with the airfield, and in the diversity of operations they carried out.

In this revision, I have drawn upon additional information, some I have researched and some supplied by locals, aviation historians and veterans, that has enabled me to tell a more complete wartime history of the base. I am especially indebted to them for their assistance and encouragement.

Of all the information uncovered, it is the stories of the men who flew from and, in some cases, diverted to RAF Beccles that have brought this book to life. Without their contributions, I doubt if this book would have been written. To them I extend a special "Thank you", and hope this publication does justice to that part of their lives, and their war, spent at RAF Beccles.

CHAPTER 1

BEGINNINGS: THE AMERICAN CONNECTION

February 1943 to August 1944

With the arrival of the 8th United States Army Air Force in East Anglia, vast areas of land were allocated for what was to become the largest building project ever undertaken in the United Kingdom. The decision to send the fledgling 8th to assault Hitler's Fortress Europe from the air was designed to test the American philosophy of massed, high altitude, precision daylight bombing, at the same time lending support to the RAF in their campaign to weaken Germany's military power. In addition to existing RAF airfields and some under construction, it was apparent that to accommodate such a huge air armada, large tracts of the fertile eastern counties would have to be allocated for airfields. In August 1942, a report detailed the requirement for 75 bomber airfields, at which time only 8 were occupied by the 8th Air Force, 10 were to be transferred from the RAF, 9 were nearing completion, and a further 12 would be completed by the end of that year. In addition, a further 28 sites had commenced construction and 8 more remained to be identified from surveyed sites.

Of the sites which remained to be identified, RAF Beccles was sited on flat, agricultural land slightly higher than the surrounding area at 80' above sea level, 2 miles to the South-East of Beccles town centre. Building work commenced in early 1943 under the direction of a London company, Holland, Hannen & Cubitt, and the airfield was designated Station 132 in the programme. The airfield itself, constructed in a Class A layout and available for use by any type of allied aircraft in service or under development, covered some 500 acres. At the time, the design of airfields required that runways were laid at approximately 60 degrees to each other, and Beccles was no exception. The main runway was built in the direction of the prevailing wind (099/279 or East/West approx) and measured 6000 X 150 feet while two more each of 4200 X 150 feet were aligned 172/352 (South/North) and 226/046 degrees (SW/NE). All were constructed in concrete. A total of 50 loop type dispersals, each designed to accommodate one or two heavy bombers, were spread around the perimeter track linking the ends of the runways. These loops were grouped in a maximum of eight, to aid dispersal and make any attacking aircraft's chances of destroying large numbers of aircraft in one pass very difficult. Two large black-painted T2 type hangars, each approximately 240 X 120 X 40 feet and able to house three heavy bombers for maintenance or repairs, were situated one on each of the East and West sides of the airfield. Near the eastern most hangar, a large earth mound provided a shooting butt where aircraft guns could be test-fired. This feature was still in place near the British International Helicopters facility until around 1970. Accommodation for a total of 2,894 people was, in the style of American rather than British airfields, widely spread over the surrounding area, requiring cycles to be issued to aircrew for transport around the site. The cost of construction totalled some £990,000 and covered such material purchases as 18,000 tons of dry cement, 90,000 tons of aggregate and 50 miles of pipework and trunking.

Beccles was built to house a Bombardment Group of 48 heavy bombers which, together with the groups from nearby Halesworth (489th) and Metfield (491st), were to form the 95th Combat Wing. Five Combat Wings constituted a Bombardment Wing, and five such formations made up the bomber element of the 8th Air Force. Bombers designated to these units would have been the well known "heavies", the Consolidated B-24 Liberator and Boeing B-17 Flying Fortress. However, with America's growing involvement in other theatres of war, diversion of resources to such places as North Africa led to a revision of building plans and allocations. With the RAF seeking further airfields in the East of England, and some US bomber airfields being allocated as maintenance and depot facilities, further changes of plan into 1943 resulted in a number of surplus airfields, one of which was Beccles. Interestingly, I heard of several other theories during my research as to why Beccles was not used by the Americans. The first was that the land was not firm enough to support the heavy bombers due to subsidence - considering Warwicks and Liberators used the airfield during the war this theory does not hold water. Nor does another that on one occasion an RAF Photographic Reconnaissance pilot, at high altitude over the French coast, could detect the movement of vehicles on the airfield. If this were the case, the RAF would not have dared base a top secret squadron at Beccles during 1944. The third, that it was too close to the coast and therefore exposed to enemy raids is flawed, since many other coastal airfields were heavily utilised for both offensive and defensive operations throughout the war years.

RAF Beccles was handed over by the controlling body, No.3 Group, RAF, to the control of the 3rd Bombardment Wing of the 8th Air Force on 25th March 1943 and onto the 4th Bombardment Wing in June. By October 1943, due to it's easterly position and proximity to returning aircraft routes, Beccles began to attract American aircraft suffering battle damage or mechanical failure, or both. During the late afternoon of November 29th, B-17 "Lady Liz" of the 550th Bomb Squadron, 385th Bomb Group, based at Great Ashfield in Suffolk, crash-landed on return from a raid on Bremen. Lieutenant Bostick's crew were luckier than some - 13 bombers and 16 fighters were lost during the raid, out of a total of over 700 participating aircraft. At that point in the war, the average life of a B-17 from the base

B-17 "Lady Liz" sits in the sugar beet field at RAF Beccles after her emergency landing on November 29th, 1943 (Ian McGlachlan/R. Zorn)

was just 4 months! The Youngs family, who at the time were living at Barber's Farm, North Cove, saw the aircraft overshoot the runway, ending up in a sugar beet field near the farm. The family recalled that the crew were very generous with souvenirs, and one member of the family came away from the scene with fifty rounds of 0.50 calibre ammunition from the B-17's formidable defensive armament.

Further visitors arrived on 20th December, when Lt Raymond B. Janney II in his Republic P-47 Thunderbolt, number 42-75141, coded CV-I, made a successful forced landing at 1235 hrs due to lack of fuel. His aircraft was from the 368th Fighter Squadron, 359th Fighter Group, at East Wretham, near Thetford, and had been escorting a large force of bombers attacking Bremen. The aircraft was subsequently lost in combat on 11th April 1944, while being flown by another pilot. Later the same day, at 1445 hrs, Lieutenant Donald Roderick nursed his crippled B-17 Fortress K22997 in to land, having had two engines damaged by enemy fire in the Bremen raid. The aircraft came from the 379th Bomb Group, based at Kimbolton in Bedfordshire. The unit went on to fly more sorties and drop a greater bomb tonnage than any other group in the 8th Air Force. The bombers had been attacked by twin engine German fighters firing rockets, in turn escorted by single engine fighters. The raid was the first where the 8th Air Force dropped 'Window', consisting of hundreds of strips of foil, to confuse the enemy's radar.

The first use by ground personnel of the 8th Air Force came in January 1944, when Squadron "M" of the 17th Replacement Control Depot were housed there during the latter stages of construction. Locals quickly struck up a rapport with the sentries on the airfield gates, and noted that although the guards carried pistols, their bandoliers only carried a handful of rounds.

Stragglers from raids continued to limp home to reach "terra firma" at Beccles. On 9th March, flak-damaged B-24H 42-7624, "Turnip Turnpike", of 578th Sqn, 392nd Bomb Group, at Wendling, Norfolk, crash-landed on return from a raid on Brandenburg. The Port main undercarriage collapsed and was ripped out of the wing, causing the aircraft to be written-off. "Turnip Turnpike" was the only one of the 392nd's 25 aircraft despatched on the raid to come to harm. On March 20th, 1944, the airfield was allocated to the 3rd Bombardment Division and occupied by an RAF Care and Maintenance party on 21st April. April was also a busy month for the emergency services on the station. Following attacks by 30 single-seat German Me-109 and FW-190 fighters during a raid on the aircraft related industrial sites at Tutow on the 9th, a battle-damaged 576th Squadron, 392nd Bomb Group B-24, serial number 42-52593, named both "Bar R" and "Lady Diana", and a 95th Bomb Group B-17, both crash-landed at Beccles. The B-24 had been hit in two engines after the group was attacked by 30 single-seat fighters, and further damaged it's undercarriage on landing. The B-17 was burnt out, but both crews escaped virtually unscathed. Bad weather disrupted the overall mission, causing delayed and aborted take-offs of some of the escort fighters, while some of the bombers were forced to abandon the raid en-route. The 576th Bomb Squadron's twelve Liberators had pressed on to the target, having missed the recall order received by the rest of the group, and had formed up with aircraft from other groups. The B-17 crash landing was again witnessed by the Youngs family, who used to watch the events unfolding on the airfield from the roof of a barn which was near the end of one runway. The crash was recalled as a "spectacular wheels up" landing, the crew abandoning the aircraft as it was still sliding to a halt on it's belly before bursting into flames and being left to burn out.

On 11th April, an emergency landing took place which, though far from typical, was a scene played out around the numerous East Anglian airfields on a daily basis. B-17F serial number 42-30793, "Tom Paine", bearing the inscription "Tyranny, like Hell, is not easily conquered", was named after a famous name in American history who was born in Thetford, close to the 388th Bomb Group's base at nearby Knettishall. The raid that day was a "maximum penetration" mission, the target for the 388th being industrial targets in the Posen area, some 65 kilometres South-East of Berlin. The plan was to fly the greater part of the mission at 12,000 ft over the North Sea and Baltic to conserve fuel, then climb to 27,000 ft at Rostock and proceed to the target. This process had the disadvantage of exposing the bombers to enemy fighters for longer, while over half the mission was flown without the protection of Allied fighter escort. From the time the formation reached the Baltic to the target, twin engine fighters harassed the bombers with long range rocket attacks. Bombers that left formation as a result of these attacks were then picked off by Messerschmitt Me109 and Focke-Wulf FW190 single engine fighters. Over the target area, the fighters backed off to allow a temporary reprieve, superseded by a fierce flak barrage. "Tom Paine's" luck held out till Rostock, when the aircraft was raked by 20mm cannon fire from a head-on attack by the ever-present fighters. The instrument panel exploded in a shower of glass and steel, while co-pilot Lieutenant Tom Copeland doubled up in his seat, wounded. The pilot of the aircraft, Lieutenant Bob McWhite, was also wounded in the leg, but managed to regain control of the aircraft with the assistance of his engineer-gunner, Sergeant Donald Winn. Although Bob's primary concern was to maintain his position in the formation for mutual protection, it quickly became obvious that this would not be possible. Maintaining his position for as long as possible, he put the aircraft into a dive and joined the formation below (bomber formations were generally "stacked" for maximum protection and to aid fields of fire). This tactic was repeated through the lower formations (to conserve fuel on the return leg) until he ran out of formations to join, then descended to between 2,000 and 3,000 ft, hoping not to be noticed by German fighters. By this time, the crew had administered morphine to Tom Copeland and moved him into the radio room. A check of the nose was discovered that the head-on attack had also wounded two other personnel in that section of the B-17, Bombardier Lieutenant Charles Tuggle and Navigator Lieutenant Clarence Adamy. The former's wounds were many superficial ones, whereas the navigator was suffering from a deep chest wound that was bubbling with blood, and could not be moved without risk of further injury and bleeding. It was determined that he would only be moved in the event of a ditching or bail out. The crew administered morphine and wrapped him in all available cover, including finally the parachutes, after the crew later opted to stay with the aircraft. Taking stock of the aircraft's condition, all engine and navigation instruments had been blown out, and the radio was dead. The crew turned on their "Identification Friend or Foe", or IFF, hoping that it still worked and that it would attract allied fighters to home in on the stricken B-17. The crew discussed heading for Sweden and interment, but the lack of navigation equipment and their exact position being unknown, led to this option being dismissed. It was decided to head first westerly and then south-westerly, hoping their over-water route would eventually take them to England. However, this was subject to the aircraft being able to maintain flight, which was by no means certain. Both inboard engines were by now trailing smoke from excessive temperature, which ordinarily could be controlled by opening the engine cowl flaps. However, the hydraulic systems which operated both these and the brakes had been punctured, witnessed by the hydraulic fluid now running beneath Bob McWhite's feet. The only option to control the engine temperatures to some level was to make the fuel mixture richer when the temperatures got too high, then making the mixture leaner when the temperatures dropped, to ensure precious fuel was conserved. After what seemed an interminable amount of time nursing both the aircraft and wounded over the open sea, two specks were spotted on the western horizon. The B-17 held it's course until they identified the two aircraft as friendly Republic P-47 Thunderbolts, which closed on either wingtip of the bomber and, by a series of hand signals, indicated they should follow the fighters. Within 10 minutes, RAF Beccles was sighted, and the difficult decision of how to land the aircraft had to be made. With inoperative brakes, a wheels up (belly) landing would normally have been the preferred method, but that would mean moving the badly wounded Adamy, which could have proved fatal. The crew decided to land with the wheels down, and attempt to ground loop the aircraft to bring it to a halt. With the Flight Engineer/Gunner Don Winn in the co-pilot's seat, the crew fired off red flares to signify wounded on board, before touching the aircraft down on the partially completed runway, narrowly missing a truck and five school children who were playing on the runway, successfully ground looping the bomber using the one application of brakes left in the hydraulic system. The bomber skewed to a halt, kicking up clods of clay, watched by the incredulous children. Ignoring them, the crew tumbled from the various hatches, carefully lifting out the wounded, including Adamy, still shrouded in the parachute silk in the exposed nose section.

The B-17 sat motionless on it's splayed undercarriage, inboard engines smoking and dripping oil and fuel, and emitting cracking noises as they cooled. As a final act of this drama, the two P-47 Thunderbolts, which had peeled away from the bomber as it made it's final approach, roared low over the scene in salute.

Bob McWhite, then 22 years old, was deservedly awarded the American Distinguished Flying Cross for bringing his crippled B-17 back to land safely, saving the entire crew. The three wounded crew members survived their ordeal, and the war. The remainder of the crew were brought up to strength with replacements, but ran out of luck in another B-17 just 13 days later, when the aircraft was shot down over Fredrikshaven, resulting in all of them parachuting into captivity for the remainder of hostilities. Placed in a Prisoner of War camp near Sagan, the crew remained there until they were marched 70 miles to a railway station at Spremburg, to avoid falling into Russian hands. They were then taken by train to Nuremburg, eventually ending up in a camp at Mooseburg, near Munich, until it was liberated by General Patton's US 3rd Army.

"Tom Paine" was later repaired and flown back to it's parent unit. The raid had attracted heavy fighter opposition, and over half of the 300 B-17s belonging to the 3rd Bombardment Division were damaged on the mission,

B-17F Fortress "Tom Paine" pictured after ground-looping following it's emergency landing at the partially completed RAF Beccles (USAAF via Christopher Elliott)

besides another 33 missing in action. "Tom Paine" was later transferred to nearby Fersfield as part of the "Aphrodite" project, involving radio controlled drone aircraft packed with high explosives, for use against such targets as heavily fortified U-boat pens. The "Aphrodite" project was to claim a famous son of America on 12th August that year, when Lt Joe Kennedy Jnr lost his life in a Fersfield based US Navy Liberator, which exploded over the coast near Southwold when it's load of 12 tons of Torpex high explosive went off without warning. This occurred as soon as the "mother" aircraft with the radio control equipment on board carried out a test of the system controlling the Liberator. That bomber was none other than "Tom Paine", which survived the war only to be flown back to the US and then melted down for scrap.

On Easter Sunday, 18th April, bombers and fighters, including B-24 Serial number 41-29150 from 705th Sqn, 446th Bomb Group, at nearby Flixton, made emergency landings on return from another mission to a German aviation component factory, but heavy clouds caused the group to bomb the secondary target of a chemical plant near Dobermitz. A widespread envelope of fog had blanketed much of the UK, causing returning aircraft to land at any available airfields. Local man Nathan Warne, who at the time lived at the western end of the main runway, counted a total of 97 aircraft, mostly B-17 and B-24s, landing on this occasion. Four days later, returning from a raid on the railway marshalling yards at Hamm in Germany, night fighters scrambled from airfields along the French coast mingled with the bomber formations in the gathering darkness, waiting for the bombers to switch on their lights to ease night formation flying. Crossing the coastline of North-East Suffolk, both American and German aircraft came under heavy anti-aircraft fire from shore batteries. All along the lower Waveney Valley, Liberators of the 2nd Air Division began falling from the skies amid the roar of Daimler-Benz and BMW engines and the staccato of cannon and machine gun fire from Messerschmitt Me410 and Junkers JU-88 night fighters. The bases of Seething, Hardwick and Flixton (Bungay) were all attacked and in the Beccles area, two Liberators fell to the ground. One, from the 467th Bomb Group at Rackheath came down near the school at Barsham, killing seven of the crew while another three baled out to safety. A memorial to the crew was erected by locals, and can be seen near the village hall alongside the B1062 that runs between Beccles and Bungay. Another B-24 of the 448th Bomb Group at Seething crashed onto the Ipswich to Lowestoft railway line at Worlingham, the crew having previously baled out. Taken by surprise at their most vulnerable, thirteen Liberators were either shot down or crash-landed during what later became known as the "Hamm Incident". RAF Beccles escaped damage in the raid, although both pursuers and pursued passed overhead, a scene witnessed from the Royal Observer Corps post on the airfield.

Bombers were not the only types to seek refuge on RAF Beccles' runways, and the first fighter recorded as making a crash-landing was a Republic P-47D Thunderbolt of the 356th Fighter Group at Martlesham Heath on 13th May. Returning from an escort mission to the Kiel area, involving 1500 aircraft, and having damaged an Fw190, the fighter landed heavily, narrowly missing a cement mixer truck working on the runway. The aircraft was written off, injuring the pilot, Lieutenant Charles W. Adams, in the process.

Tremendous damage to the bombers often failed to knock them out of the sky, as B-17G "Mary Alice", serial number 42-31983, of the 615th Bomb Squadron, 401st Bomb Group, at Deenethorpe, proved on 13th July. Built at the end of 1943, she was one of the last B-17's to emerge from Boeing's Seattle factory painted in olive drab and grey. "Mary Alice", squadron code IY-G, was named after the mother of the first pilot assigned to the B-17, Lieutenant Dan C. Knight. He and his crew completed 30 missions, before handing over the aircraft to other crews. Part of a daylight "thousand bomber" raid on the aero engine works at Munich, with other targets at Stuttgart and on the rail marshalling yards at Saarbrucken, the bombers were once again frustrated by weather. A front reached up to 29,000' in places, making visual bombing very difficult. The 401st provided the low, exposed, box position in the 94th Combat Wing formation. One of 200

The tail gunner's position of B-17 "Mary Alice", devastated by cannon fire, pictured in a hangar at RAF Beccles (Dan Knight)

bombers damaged on the mission, "Mary Alice" came under attack from 15-20 fighters in her exposed position at the rear of the group. Two fighters attacked from astern, while a further one came in from high on the port wing. Cannon shells exploded in the vicinity of the number 2 engine, knocking out the turbo supercharger, also hitting the bomb bay, the port wing near the root and one fuel tank, with further shells wrecking the left tailplane and tail gunner's position.

The order was given to bail out, only for it to be rescinded when it was realised that the bail out alarm and intercom were not functioning properly and the tail gunner was mortally wounded. Twenty year old Sergeant Edward L Page had been hit by 20mm cannon-shells, one hitting him in the chest, but remained in his tail position firing his guns, and was credited with the destruction of at least one Fw190 before succumbing to his injuries. He was awarded the posthumous Silver Star for his gallantry. The aircraft started to spin, but was brought back under control, and the crew nursed the aircraft back for a successful emergency landing at RAF Beccles with little fuel remaining. Before landing the pilot, 2nd Lieutenant Harry Haskett, had the crew fire off red Very lights to attract attention on the largely deserted airfield. Under an agreement with the USAAF Medical

Officer at nearby RAF Halesworth, a Beccles doctor, believed to be Dr Grantham-Hill, attended the scene and gave aid to the dying tail gunner. "Mary Alice" flew a total of at least 98 combat missions by VE-day, and by that time was believed to have the dubious "honour" of the 8th Air Force B-17 sustaining the most damage and still remain in service. Though the 401st Bomb Group did not suffer the huge losses of many other groups, "Mary Alice" always seemed to be in the thick of it and rarely escaped a mission without some damage or mishap. She survived the war, flying back to the USA, where she was scrapped in November 1945.

Though a sad end to an aircraft that had seen at least one crew safely through their 30 mission tour of duty, a static B-17 at the Imperial War Museum, Duxford, is preserved in her colours as a fitting tribute to the thousands of young airman who fought and died in such aircraft.

Another bomber to seek refuge at Beccles was "Lonesone Lois", a B-24H, serial number 42-95020 X+, of the 701st Bomb Squadron, 445th Bomb Group, based at Tibenham, Norfolk. On landing, the aircraft finished up on a grass area, where the nose wheel collapsed. The incident was reported on 13th July, suggesting the aircraft was most likely one of 1,271 to hit Munich the previous day. The aircraft was repaired by 8th August, and went on to survive the war, only to end up in the aircraft graveyard at Altus, and scrap metal thereafter.

If returning bombers were a hazard to the local populace, outward bound ones were a positive menace. A Handley Page Halifax of 578 Sqn, RAF, did it's utmost to change the local landscape on the night of 3rd August. With a 22 ft long bomb bay capable of carrying up to 13,000 lbs of bombs, the aircraft had developed an elevator problem which became serious enough for the crew to abandon it. The Halifax came down near the junction of Banham Road and Coney Hill, Beccles, narrowly avoiding nearby houses. The resulting explosion of bomb load and fuel left a large crater in the ground, though miraculously without inflicting injury.

One of the "celebrities" to visit RAF Beccles, though not strictly by choice, was Major John T. "Johnny" Godfrey, commanding officer of the 336th Fighter Squadron, 4th Fighter Group, USAAF, operating out of Debden in Essex. As "wingman" to ace Don Gentile, who ended the war with 22 victories, the pair had developed an excellent partnership, employing the unconventional tactic of allowing whoever spotted the enemy first and was in the best position, to take the lead to attack the enemy, the other partner covering his tail. The tactic was so successful that it was used by American fighter pilots many years later in the Vietnam war.

Their combination was so effective that the head of the Luftwaffe, Hermann Goring, is said to have sworn he would have given up two squadrons for their capture. John Godfrey had already shot down a Messerschmitt Me410 on 6th August, as part of a large raid of 1,186 bombers and 740 fighters to attack oil refineries, aircraft ordnance and

B-24H Liberator "Lonesome Lois" after her emergency landing at RAF Beccles on 13th July 1944 (USAF, via Steve Adams)

other factories in Germany, as well as V-weapon sites in France. As he led his squadron in a strafing attack on an enemy airfield, where he claimed another five enemy aircraft destroyed, his Mustang's engine was hit by anti-aircraft fire, resulting in a coolant leak. Preparing to abandon his red-nosed P-51D number 44-13412 (coded VF-P), he was advised by another group "ace", Fred Glover, to use the priming pump to inject neat fuel into the engine and thereby lower the temperature. Despite a small wound on his forehead, and his hand chaffed raw through constant priming for two and a half hours, Godfrey brought the aircraft as far as the first airfield sighted on reaching the English coast. Escorted by another Mustang, his aircraft, named both "Lucky" after his dog and "Reggies Reply" after his air mechanic brother, who was lost in the North Atlantic when his vessel was torpedoed by a U-boat earlier in the war, made a safe emergency landing at Beccles. Afterwards, he returned to duty, but was captured when his aircraft was shot down by what is now known as "friendly fire" during another airfield attack eighteen days later.

By now it had been decided to hand RAF Beccles to 16 Group, Coastal Command, a handover which was officially recorded in the Station Log as occurring on 14th August 1944. The RAF had recognised the advantages of the airfield's proximity to the newly opened bombing range at Wells-next-the-Sea, and the fact that the airfield was empty, as the base was about to welcome it's most secretive residents.

CHAPTER 2

MOST SECRET SQUADRON

August to October 1944

Fact is often stranger than fiction, it is said. This was never more so than in the case of 618 Squadron, Royal Air Force. When Coastal Command took over Beccles as an operational flying station on 14th August, it was for the purpose of specialist training for a project which, had it been implemented in it's original form, have been remembered today as an achievement alongside the Dams Raid. To put the period of residence at Beccles in proper context, it is necessary to briefly chart the previous history of 618 Sqn and "Highball".

Formed at Skitten on 1st April 1943 from elements of 105 and 139 Squadrons, with the formidable and versatile De Havilland Mosquito B.Mk IV, the Squadron was a "sister" unit to what became the best known Squadron of the RAF, 617. Part of a double blow to Hitler's war machine, one half was codenamed "Upkeep", which became what is now described as the "bouncing bomb" made famous by the Dams raid. The second part of this hammer blow was codenamed "Highball", and was designed to be delivered on the day preceding the Dams raid. Both weapons were in fact not "bouncing bombs" at all, but spinning mines, both designed to be delivered at low altitude over water, both spun backwards to accentuate the bouncing effect. Having struck their targets and sunk alongside, they were to be detonated at a pre-determined depth by a hydrostatic pistol to create a shock wave, destroying their targets. Though similar in principal, Highball was by far the smaller weapon, more spherical than it's bigger relative, and intended as an anti-shipping weapon. Even so, it could deliver a far greater punch than any air-launched torpedo. The prestige of destroying the Dams on one night, following 618 sinking the mighty German battleship "Tirpitz", supposedly safe behind anti-submarine nets and booms in a Norwegian fjord, can only have been imagined. The fear of the allies was that separate attacks on the Dams and the vessel would alert the Germans to the weapon and result in them modifying the Titpitz's boom defence to neutralise the effect. However, the Dams raid was very much dependent upon the water levels being high, and so, unlike the Tirpitz attack, could not be postponed. The Tirpitz, at a standard displacement of 42,900 tonnes, was the largest battleship ever built in Europe, and her main armament of eight 15 inch guns, coupled with a top speed of over 30 knots, made her a formidable adversary. Winston Churchill dubbed her "The Beast", and after her sister ship, the Bismark, had sunk the battle-cruiser HMS Hood in a matter of minutes, it was decreed that a minimum force of two King George V class battleships and an aircraft carrier would be needed before Tirpitz could be engaged at sea. Her very presence threatened the Arctic convoys to Russia, and in 1942 intelligence that she had sailed resulted in the order to scatter the 33 ships of convoy PQ-17, over two thirds of which were then sunk by German U-boats and aircraft. Though damaged by midget submarines of the Royal Navy in September 1943, and again by dive bombers of the Fleet Air Arm in April 1944, her very existence tied up three modern British battleships in home waters in case she broke out into the open sea again. However, the Mosquito was only selected to carry the new weapon late in the day, and it wasn't until March 1943 that an example was modified to carry the mines. Trials quickly followed with wooden and steel cased weapons, but release mechanism failures and lack of practice time led to the date for the raid being postponed. With trials continuing through to early September, 618 were suddenly told to move their aircraft into storage, just as the weapons were beginning to perform as expected. This improvement in performance led to the order being rescinded and the Squadron moved to Wick in Scotland to continue training. By early 1944, it became apparent that the Mosquitoes would need Merlin 25 engines to achieve the desired low-level performance. Detachments were made to other Squadrons in an attempt to boost crew morale, which had suffered from the long period developing the weapon, until the unit was brought back together at Wick in July 1944. By this time, the War Cabinet had decided that Tirpitz no longer justified the use of "Highball". Other targets were being considered, as the "Tirpitz" was still seriously damaged from an earlier raid and been moved North, out of range of UK-based Mosquitoes. Unbeknown to the allies, a hit from a 9 Squadron Lancaster on the bow of the vessel on 15th September rendered her unserviceable for sea, and as she could not realistically be moved to a large dock, Tirpitz was allocated the role of a floating gun battery and moved further south to Tromso. Ironically, she was destined to succumb to another weapon from the Barnes-Wallis armoury. For all her defences, and after a raid by Lancasters of 617 Sqn with massive 12,000 lb "Tallboy" bombs, she was dealt a mortal blow and finally capsized on November 12th, 11 minutes after receiving the first direct hit.

"Highball" had already been considered for other uses - as conventional mines, for use against u-boat pens, anti-tank walls in France, and even as stores to be bounced into the entrance of tunnels! In the latter role, test drops were carried out in a tunnel in Derbyshire, a third of the stores running the length of the tunnel. The targets being considered for such an eccentric scheme were the road tunnels linking Italy and Europe, and those used for storing V-1 rockets, but this was to prove yet another red herring in the development of Highball. Next, the Italian Fleet were to be delivered a knockout blow to prevent the vessels falling into the hands of the Germans, but before this idea got off the ground the Italians surrendered to the Allies. The latest plan to be tabled was considered both politically and militarily a "most important contribution to the war against Japan", and involved a mass attack by 21 Mosquitoes on the enemy capital ships operating in the area of Singapore, Borneo and the Phillipines, under the codename of operation "Oxtail". It was known that there were at least five battleships and nine aircraft carriers in this zone, and to justify the exposure of the weapon to the enemy at least a third of these ships had to be in one port for the raid to take place. Due to the lack of suitable land-based airfields within range of the enemy ports, it would be necessary for the raid to be launched from aircraft carriers, so among the modifications carried out by Marshalls at Cambridge and Airspeed of Portsmouth were the fitting of arrester hooks. Besides these, the uprated Merlin 25 engines and the modifications necessary to house, sight and release the stores, the aircraft were fitted with air turbines and motive power for spinning the mines, as well as armour plating and armoured windscreens for additional protection against anti-aircraft fire.

RAF Beccles became the home of 618 Sqn when the first of their aircraft arrived on 13th August 1944, with the remaining aircraft arriving between 23rd and 25th of that month. Most of the aircraft consisted of Mosquito B.Mk IVs, with a few PR Mk VIs with which to reconnoitre enemy ports, but in addition two Avro Anson training and communication aircraft and a single Supermarine Spitfire arrived to take up residence. By 14th August the station establishment was made up of 21 Officers, 181 Airmen and 116 WAAFs, all commanded by Group Captain R.C.Keary. When 618 Sqn had completed their move, a further 188 men were added to the complement. The squadron quickly settled into their new surroundings, using an aircraft carrier deck marked on the runway to continue the practice of Aerodrome Dummy Deck Landings (ADDLs), in preparation for their operation at sea. This exercise was given added authenticity by the "loan" of a Fleet Air Arm 'Batman' to guide the aircraft onto the imaginary deck.

All this activity was carried out under the greatest secrecy, although spectators were frequently spotted on nearby roads outside the perimeter taking an interest in the proceedings. One such spectator recalled spending many Saturday mornings watching the Mosquitoes from the Mutford side of the airfield, but never being given sight of a "Highball" slung in one of the faired open bomb-bays. A Navigator with 618 Sqn at the time recalled wondering what the spectators made of it all, and whether any of them were enemy spies. The top secret nature of the project was such that talk of the weapon outside the base was strictly forbidden. The allied high command's paranoia was well founded, since the weapon in enemy hands offered them far more potential targets. Indeed, the day after the Dams raid, an unexploded example of "Upkeep" was recovered by the Germans, who developed a weapon far more akin to "Highball", known as the Kurt Bouncing Bomb. The spherical weapon, weighing 850lb and rocket-assisted, was designed to jettison the rocket on contact with the water,

De Havilland Mosquito B.Mk IV releases a "Highball" spinning mine during a low level practice drop. (British Aerospace)

bounce for up to 500 yards, then sink alongside the target and explode at a certain depth via hydrostatic fuse. It was extensively tested, initially underneath a Messerschmitt Me410, then with two slung under the belly of a Focke-Wulf Fw190, but the project was cancelled before the weapon was used in anger. Even in 1945, when the De Havilland company made a film about the Mosquito, the "Highball" project was the only aspect of the aircraft's development which for security reasons had to be excluded.

The level of security at Beccles was heightened still further with the arrival of a detachment of Special Police for duty with the squadron early in September. Local man Les Baldry, on leave from instructing trainees in the art of air gunnery and navigation, decided to take a closer look at a Mosquito, never having seen one before at close quarters. Borrowing his brother's bicycle, he set out wearing his RAF 'Blues', travelling up a side road to the airfield perimeter. Eventually he spotted a Mosquito parked on a hardstanding about 50 yards from a five bar gate on the airfield boundary. Pulling in to lean on the gate and take in the features of the aircraft, he was startled by the sudden appearance of an RAF Policeman who popped up from behind the hedge and demanded to know what Les was doing there. After scrutinising his identity card, Les was told in no uncertain terms to 'clear off', as nobody was allowed to linger near this part of the airfield.

At the beginning of September training intensified, with a detachment of Mosquitoes sent to RAF Turnberry, Ayrshire, for dummy attacks against a "live" target. HMS Malaya, a battleship which had just returned from bombarding operations in support of the D-Day landings and subsequent push into France, was moored in Loch Striven and listed to port so that any impact of stores would be absorbed by the armour plate on her side. The

Mosquitoes would aim their runs to be at 360 mph, 50-60 feet above the water. The air turbine would spin the two mines at 1,000 revs via a belt drive, the crew releasing the mines at 3 second intervals, 1200 yards from the target. On 15th September the new range at Wells-next-the-Sea was used for the first time, when 68 stores were dropped to be later recovered at low tide for inspection. In addition, the bow and stern of a vessel were marked across the end of one runway at Beccles, the runway graduated at intervals, with dummy drops of sashlight bulbs to verify the length of run and drop height. Seventy-three of these exercises were carried out during the month with encouraging results. Distinguished visitors arrived at Beccles on 20th September in the form of Admiral Renouf and a Mr Barnes Wallis CBE. Navigator Leon Murray, then with 618 Sqn, remembered being lectured on Operation Oxtail and seeing Barnes-Wallis chalking a very complicated algebraic equation on the blackboard. He added that "None of us could understand it, but never-the-less he was a very impressive personality".

Such intensive low level training, with crews who had been preparing themselves for many months, could not be achieved without a certain accident rate. Taking off from RAF North Coates on a training exercise, Mk VI PZ295, flown by Flying Officer D.G. Maddocks, suffered a wheels up landing after both throttles slipped back on take-off and control was lost after a swing developed. En-route from another dummy attack on HMS Malaya on 26th September, one Mosquito force landed at Thornaby, Yorkshire, on one engine. Back at Beccles the squadron "hack", Spitfire JF286, was taxiing after landing when the port tyre burst, slewing the aircraft off the runway onto the grass and causing it to tip onto it's nose. As September closed 618 Sqn had flown 387 sorties totalling 578 hours in the air, and having dropped 68 stores on the range at Wells. Despite this, Squadron members still found time to relax in the "traditional" RAF way in a local hostelry, usually the "Horse & Groom". They also took the opportunity to try out their inflatable dinghies by jumping off the bridge over the river Waveney to make sure they worked properly, much to the amusement of the locals. October was to see the final preparations for embarkation to the Far East, with detachments to RAF Turnberry for further weapons trials from the 2nd to 13th, while on 8th three PR crews took their aircraft to Wick to prepare for deck landing trials on HMS Implacable in Scapa Flow. Crews had already practised deck landings on HMS Rajah using Barracuda aircraft borrowed from the Fleet Air Arm, most of which weren't returned in the same state! To assist crews to undertake the hazardous operation of landing a fast, twin-engine aircraft on a small, moving deck, the Squadron was visited at Beccles by Lt. Cdr. Eric M. (Winkle) Brown, who had the distinction of being the first man to land a twin-engined aircraft (also a Mosquito) on the moving deck of an aircraft carrier in May 1944. During his visit, he noted a Mosquito in one of the hangars "with a strange object peeping out of the bomb-bay", but despite the presence of Barnes Wallis, he never guessed the reason for his mission to instruct in the art of deck landing.

It was during one of the detachments to Turnberry that the most serious accident to befall 618 Sqn during it's stay at Beccles took place. While trying to break cloud over Bramsdale, Yorkshire, Mosquito Mk IV DZ648 crashed into hills, destroying the aircraft and killing both crew members, Flight Sergeant E.A. Stubbs and Warrant Officer A.R.W. Milne. The area was quickly secured and under the direction of Special Police the weapons were removed under great secrecy. Further aircraft modifications, including the fitting of radio altimeters and fluxgate compasses were made at Beccles in readiness for the loading onto carriers. The Fleet Air Arm airfield at Crail in Scotland was also utilised for deck landing practice, using the dummy carrier deck there. In late September, the battleship HMS Malaya arrived in Loch Striven, and was ballasted to expose the lower part of the ship's hull to the practice stores, and to protect damage to the upper hull, which was protected by thinner armour. Detaching again to RAF Turnberry, the Mosquitoes carried out dummy attacks into early October, sometimes during adverse weather and dropping the stores into waves up to 15' high. The final attacks were carried out on 12th October, when 2 of the 3 "Highballs" dropped penetrated the thinner part of the hull aft, one into the wardroom and the second into the Admiral's pantry, ruining the food stored there. By way of a parting shot, it had been planned for a mass dummy attack by the whole squadron on the fleet at Scapa Flow, but owing to the lack of time and the accident risk the idea was dropped. However, the performance of the crews and the stores had impressed the Chiefs of Staff, to the point that a second "Highball" equipped Squadron was considered. By 28th October the Squadron's 24 B.MkIV and 3 MkVI aircraft had been loaded aboard the carriers HMS Striker and HMS Fencer in Glasgow Docks. The following day, a special train was laid on to take the remaining personnel of 618 Sqn, numbering 363 personnel, from Beccles to the King George V dock, Glasgow, ending the unit's association with RAF Beccles.

Subsequently, the squadron was posted to Australia, where the wait for action continued, the Japanese capital ships becoming fewer and further away as the months passed. There was also some reluctance by the Americans to use the weapon in what was essentially "their" theatre of war. Finally, on 29th June 1945, it was announced that the Squadron was to be disbanded, an announcement that was charted in the unit's record book as a "shock to all ranks". By now two more crews had met violent deaths in training accidents, victims in part to the frustration of endless training without going into action. The final act in the "secret" squadron's history was the explosion of all the live stores they had brought with them, for security reasons. The explosion of 125 "Highballs" at the Royal Australian Navy Depot at Auburn was said to have rattled windows in Sydney, causing consternation with the residents, and ensuring the unit "went out with a bang".

During October only one American aircraft sought refuge at RAF Beccles. On the second of the month, a battle-damaged 489th Bomb Group Liberator, operating out of nearby Halesworth, crash landed with one dead crew member on board following a raid on the Hamm marshalling yards. The raid saw 2 of the 308 B-24's despatched lost, with a further 2 damaged beyond repair and another 144 damaged to some degree.

Before 618 Sqn departed RAF Beccles, three more Squadron contingents made only brief stays at the airfield. Flying two biplane types, 119 Sqn RAF with five Fairey Albacores and 819 Sqn Fleet Air Arm with five Fairey Swordfish arrived on 13th September to begin anti-shipping operations that night. Owing to adverse weather only three aircraft made it off the ground, and the following day 16 Group, to whom the units were assigned, cancelled the operation and all aircraft left for Swingfield, near Dover, to carry out similar duties in the English Channel. The anti-shipping theme continued in the form of seventeen ungainly Fairey Barracuda Mk III's of 827 Sqn FAA, which arrived from RNAS Crail in Fife on 15th October, under the command of Lt. Cdr. G.R. Woolston. These aircraft, like the Swordfish and Albacore, were designed for carrier operations, and found a new lease of life in the shore-based anti-shipping role.

827 Sqn had seen a good deal of action earlier in 1944, sharing hits on the mighty "Tirpitz" during the raid in March 1944, and taking part in further raids in July and August. Absorbing another unit involved in the first raid, 830 Sqn, the unit transferred from HMS Furious, via RNAS Hatston in the Orkneys, with the task of attacking enemy ships sailing off the Dutch coast. This had been determined because the squadron's next carrier, HMS Colossus, suffered a serious fire in dry-dock on the Tyne and the unit was offered to Coastal Command while the damage was repaired. Once at Beccles, the unit split into two flights, embarking on navigation exercises and practice dive-bombing during the day, returning to operate from Langham at night. The reason for this was that Beccles was close to the coastal belt of anti-flying bomb gun units, and it was soon apparent that the split between two bases was impractical. Because of the limited range of the Barracudas and the necessary diversion round the barrage area, the time left on patrol was considered too short to be worthwhile. An observer with the squadron at the time, Nelson Abraham, recalled that "anything flying in the barrage area below 6,000 feet was automatically clobbered". On 28th October, the Squadron moved back to Langham, from where it went into action against enemy "E-boats" the following month. Not all the Fleet Air Arm personnel moved out immediately, however. The RAF Squadron Leader in charge of the Operations Room at RAF Beccles had requested Duty Signals Officers from the FAA to act as liaison with the RAF. Consequently, three newly qualified Observers were posted to the Ops

Room in October, just before the Barracudas moved out. Setting up the Signals Office as ordered, the three were remembered by the Admiralty after a couple of weeks and moved on to more gainful employ. Before they left and during off duty periods, the trio "scrounged" lifts in the latest aircraft to arrive at Beccles, which were destined to become the station's longest residents during the war.

CHAPTER 3

THE RESCUERS

November 1944

*"Glory, Glory, may you never come down in the sea,
Bugger your luck, my boy, if you're there relying on me,
I would rather be here ashore than swimming from
there with thee,
Because you've had it chum."
(Mess song, sung to the tune of John Brown's Body)*

Few people who have seen the bright yellow painted Seaking helicopters of the modern RAF Air Sea Rescue (ASR) squadrons are aware of their origins, which date back to the dark days of 1940.

During the Battle of Britain, only one in ten of the allied fighter and bomber aircrew who "ditched" into the English Channel were rescued, those fortunate to do so being recovered by one of a few RAF High Speed Launches. The Luftwaffe, on the other hand, employed Heinkel floatplanes to supplement their launches, speed being of the essence when saving life from the cold, clutching waters. The RAF woke up to this waste of their valuable aircrew late in 1940 when, as well as doubling the number of rescue launches, aircraft began to be employed for spotting ditched crews and dropping dinghies, supplies and survival equipment. Initially, the aircraft employed were Westland Lysanders, unemployable in their usual role of army co-operation since the fall of France. Aided by the formation of an Air Sea Rescue Directorate in January 1941, the additional resources caused the survival rate to jump to 33% after only six months of the Directorate's formation. Other aircraft types started appearing in the ASR role, fast Supermarine Spitfire IIs and Boulton Paul Defiants for spotting, dropping floats and keeping the area clear of enemy vessels and aircraft, which were now beginning to interfere with rescue operations. From the employment of shore-based Fleet Air Arm units, the idea came to impress the Supermarine Walrus amphibian aircraft into the ASR role, allowing rapid recovery of crews suffering from injury or hypothermia. With the emphasis on offensive action as the war progressed, the ASR organisation grew in size, although in East Anglia the only base initially offering this facility was Martlesham Heath, near Ipswich. Soon Coltishall, Horsham St Faiths and Bircham Newton in Norfolk received ASR units, an expansion which continued in line with the increase in the bomber offensive and arrival of the USAAF in East Anglia. Longer ranges resulting from the variety of targets, and diversions flown to avoid heavy flak concentrations and to confuse the enemy, meant that larger aircraft with greater endurance and more sophisticated survival equipment were required. Twin engine types such as Avro Ansons, Lockheed Hudsons and Vickers Warwicks were increasingly used, concurrent with the development of new technology in survival aids. Early trials of Hudsons with a unique parachute-delivered wooden lifeboat, complete with engine, led to a larger model being carried under the fuselage of Warwick, a practice which went into full operation from August 1943. Flying from Langham, Norfolk, the first unit to receive the unique combination was 280 Squadron, RAF. 280 Squadron had been formed as an Air Sea Rescue unit at Thorney Island on the South coast, later moving to Detling. Regular redeployment around the coastal airfields of East Anglia and Southern England resulted in the squadron finding residence at RAF Beccles, arriving there on 29th October and commencing patrols the following day with their Warwick ASR Mk I's and II's. As one of the most Easterly airfields in the area, Beccles was ideally placed to provide rapid assistance in the form of ASR aircraft far out over the North Sea, over which thousands of allied bombers were now flying every day and night.

The lumbering Warwicks had been designed to complement rather than replace the Vickers Wellington, a type to which it closely resembled. Resulting from the poorer than expected performance of the high-power engine designs, and an emphasis on four-engine bomber designs for improved performance and bomb load, the Warwick was to prove but a shadow of it's sibling. Limited by the RAF's hangar dimensions, and based on the complex but rugged Geodetic construction designed by Barnes-Wallis, the aircraft was designed to be powered by two 1,000 hp engines with variable pitch propellers. After several changes to specification, power plant, and problems with construction, the prototype finally flew for the first time on 13th August 1939. Weighing in at a hefty 13 tons, the Warwick was capable of carrying 7,500 lbs of bombs over a range of 2,000 miles at economic cruising speed. A crew of seven was specified, including air gunners to operate the three Frazer-Nash power operated turrets in the nose, tail and mid-upper positions, each with twin .303 Browning machine guns.

The development of airborne lifeboats was not seriously considered by the Air Ministry until 1942, by which time the designer, Lieutenant Robb RN, had met up with a well known yacht designer, Uffa Fox.
Experimentation began, using a Lockheed Hudson as a launch vehicle. When the Warwick became available Uffa Fox decided the MkI lifeboat could be re-designed into a larger and more effective model, the 1A fitted with an inboard Austin 10 automobile engine and constructed of American Rock Elm and Honduras Mahogany. The 30 ft long boat, weighing 3,600 lbs, was designed to be dropped using between three and six parachutes normally configured in a single group. The 'chutes were attached so that the boat would strike the water at 30 degrees, lessening the chance of breaking up on impact. Canopies at either end of the boat would be inflated by CO_2

chambers on contact with the water, righting the boat. Water-activated rockets fired automatically from the sides of the boat to deploy buoyant ropes helped the downed aircrews intercept it, while the parachutes automatically detached, again with the aid of immersion switches. Possessing a range of almost 500 miles, the lifeboats were equipped with exposure suits, medical supplies, hot water bags, food, water-purifying units and cigarettes.

It is fair to say that the USAAF in 1942 were in a similar, if not worse state than the RAF in 1940, with very little thought and even less resources allocated to Air Sea Rescue. The American bomber and fighter aircraft often had obsolete and ineffective survival aids, besides which the poor ditching characteristics of the Liberators and early Fortresses did nothing for crew morale. Although some Thunderbolt fighters, equipped with smoke flares and under-wing four-man dinghy packs, were allocated for ASR duties during 1942, it wasn't until January 1945 that OA-10 Catalina flying boats arrived at Halesworth, shortly followed by half a dozen war weary Fortresses equipped with Higgins A-1 lifeboats. In the interim period, the burden of ASR support for the American flyers fell to the RAF.

The arrival of 280 Sqn at Beccles brought the station complement up to around 450 personnel, a quarter of whom were WAAFs. The Warwick crews were, for the most part, drawn from experienced aircrew with at least one tour "under their belts", leading to a happy atmosphere and a relaxed attitude to training. Arriving by train shortly after the squadron transferred Andy Padbury, a young Wireless Operator/Air Gunner, was advised to concentrate on gunnery practice for a few days by a wily Gunnery Leader who casually confessed to having lost three aircraft in the fortnight prior to the move from Langham. Andy was relieved to discover that the Squadron was highly regarded by Group Headquarters for the aircrew's level of experience. Many of them had expressed a wish to remain on operations after completing tours of duty on bombers, which gave Andy some measure of comfort with his posting. They were a very mixed bunch - South Africans, Canadians, Americans on loan from the USAAF, Australians and New Zealanders, all rotating continually as tours came to an end. Some had flown in a wide range of aircraft types. For example, Flight Mechanic/Air Gunner 'Gus' Platts flew in Whitley bombers during 1940, moving onto Defiant fighters, Sunderland and Catalina flying boats before taking up the tail gunners position in 280's Warwicks. Some of the aircrew had transferred from another Air Sea Rescue Squadron, 282, and brought along their experience to ease the burden for the members of 280 Squadron.

The posting of experienced crews to the squadron was no accident, as Air Sea Rescue aircraft were required to fly long sorties in a hostile nvironment, often unescorted, in weather that kept most other units firmly on the ground. Their main employment was to accompany outgoing daylight bomber raids, loitering off the Dutch coast to escort returning

Vickers Warwick ASR Mk I of 280 Sqn, with Mark IA lifeboat underslung (Imperial War Museum, Neg MH5334)

stragglers or drop survival equipment to those which couldn't reach the East Anglian coast and which were forced to ditch in the North Sea. Joining the bomber stream off Southwold, the lone Warwicks flew at 4,000 feet, well below the bombers and close enough to the water to administer rapid assistance. Arriving off the enemy-occupied coast, the heavily loaded Warwick with it's cumbersome 30 foot lifeboat slung underneath was vulnerable to fighter attack, so two or three allied fighters were usually tasked with providing protection during this stage of the operation. Far from giving comfort to the Warwick crews, the opposite effect was sometimes experienced when the escorting American Mustang pilots decided to have a natter about anything and everything, which happened regularly. On other occasions the escorts, low on fuel, announced their departure with a "Cheerio, Good Luck" message - fortunately the Luftwaffe were too occupied with the main bomber force to be concerned with a lone Warwick which bore them no threat, despite the latter's apparent attempt to draw attention to itself! Back at Beccles certain aircraft were kept on immediate readiness, positioned on dispersal hardstandings near the end of the duty runway, their crews sleeping in caravans adjacent to their aircraft. These would be "scrambled" on receipt of a call notifying a ditching where no immediate naval cover was available, the airborne assistance being of vital importance to locate and aid the unfortunate airmen. The latest meteorological information was relayed to the caravans from operations, along with regular supplies of food from the mess. Crews on operations could expect to be in this 'standby' role one day, the following one at the bottom of a list of up to twenty available crews, the first three of which could be in the air. The second and third crews on the list would remain in the mess, fourth on camp, and so on, those at the very bottom being able to enjoy a trip to Yarmouth or Lowestoft, visit the cinema in Beccles or go sailing on the Waveney. In the last respect, airborne lifeboats were sometimes used, ostensibly to carry out boat testing, though not all trips turned out as expected. On one occasion, Andy Padbury and three friends fell foul of the changeable local weather when on a nautical expedition to Lowestoft. With the wind rising to a gale, and assailed by alternate lashings of rain, sleet, hail and snow in rapid succession, they tried to turn back to Beccles, only succeeding in taking on copious amounts of water and getting soaked themselves. Finally getting both sail and mast down, they managed to get the engines going and made it back to Beccles, much the wiser for their experience! The adventure didn't deter others from taking to the Waveney, and many a pleasant hour was spent by airmen during the squadron's stay at Beccles, making sure the lifeboats were "fully operational".

The first success came quickly for 280 Sqn, when dinghy-equipped Warwick "G-George" located the survivors of a downed RAF Lancaster on 14th November, the five crew members being rescued by a trawler operating in the area. By now the crews were into the routine of three to five hour sorties flown on a daily basis, rotating the aircraft to allow for regular maintenance. Mud was a constant problem in the damp autumn weather, and on 26th November Flight Sergeant Queffers overshot the runway on landing his Warwick, which sank knee deep in it. Aircrew and ground crew alike spent all the next day digging it out, before it was towed away for repair. "Queff", as the unfortunate pilot was known to his pals, was a transferee from 282 Sqn, another Air Sea Rescue unit, and was universally liked despite his habit of holding the Warwick on the runway way above take-off speed, only to pull up at the end of the runway and make an immediate sharp turn, with the inboard wingtip almost touching the ground. Andy Padbury started flying with his new crew, including a pilot who carried an injury from a bomber raid earlier in the war. Taking off, his leg gave way, causing the aircraft to veer onto the grass and finally get airborne alongside one of the hangers. Unperturbed and laughing, his only comment was "What's all the panic, chaps, we're airborne aren't we?" During November, the Officer Commanding the Group visited RAF Beccles, but was furious with the unserviceability he found. Out of twenty four aircraft only two, the "Scramble" aircraft at the end of the duty runway and the standby aircraft positioned near the mess, were serviceable. Worse was to follow. Half-way down the runway, one engine on the scramble aircraft stopped, the pilot narrowly avoiding an embarrassing overshoot into the mud. Ten minutes later, the standby Warwick broke down at the end of the runway as it was about to begin it's take-off run. This episode signalled the end for the unreliable Bristol Centaurus equipped Warwick Mk IIs, which were replaced by American Pratt and Whitney Double Wasps shortly after.

The weather continued to have a big influence on operations from the bomber stations, and on 5th November the station played host to visiting Fortresses of the 351st Bomb Group from Polebrook, Northamptonshire, which had diverted on return from a 452 aircraft strong raid on marshalling yards at Frankfurt due to high winds and rain. Another aircraft participating on the raid was a 93rd Bomb Group Liberator from Hardwick, Norfolk. Attempting to make it back to it's home base, most of the crew having already opted to bail out, the aircraft fell to the ground at Shipmeadow, killing the remaining two members on board. After conditions had improved, the Fortresses prepared to leave, but were somewhat delayed on take-off because the pilots couldn't understand the instructions relayed from the control tower. It turned out the chap on the other end of the radio possessed a pronounced Oxford accent, and matters were only resolved when the senior American officer present took over the tower radio himself to relay instructions to the waiting bombers.

During November one of the most tragic happenings on the base occurred, one which most locals who lived in the area at the time still recall as the single enduring memory of the airfield's history.

CHAPTER 4

MURDER IN GREEN LANE

Among the hundreds of thousands of Allied deaths during the Second World War, the death of a single WAAF might seem like a drop in the ocean to all but her friends and relatives. However, the addition of a criminal element to the event focuses attention which can survive long after the "main event" has ended.

Amid a flying bomb attack on the east coast, and during the wettest November for four years, twenty-seven year old WAAF Winifred Mary Evans spent the evening of Wednesday 8th November away from her station at RAF Beccles, attending one of the regular dances held at local American airfields. Hailing from Harlesden in West London, she had many friends and enjoyed her job as a wireless operator, despite the sadness of losing a brother in the Western Desert and both parents during the war. Due on duty at 11.30 pm, she returned to the female billets at RAF Beccles, changed, and ventured out into the cold, dark lane which led to the headquarters building. Shortly after, a drunk RAF Corporal was found loitering near the female billets by a WAAF and sent on his way, heading down the same dark lane that Winifred had recently taken. The Corporal, Arthur Heys, from Colne in Lancashire, was a thirty-seven year old married man with three young children. Well liked by both men and women on the station, he seemed the embodiment of a happily married father, making toys in the workshops for his children most evenings. He too had attended a dance that evening, this time in nearby Beccles town, although his evening had been somewhat spoiled by discovering his bicycle had been "borrowed", requiring him to walk back to his billet on the base. At 8.00 am the following morning, a local civilian found Winifred's body in a ditch by the junction of Green Lane and Ellough Road. She had been raped and assaulted, her face pushed into the mud at the bottom of the ditch, where she suffocated. Because of the large number of service and civilian suspects, as well as Italian prisoners-of-war held in a local camp, and due to the nature of the murder, it was decided to call in Scotland Yard. While they were still en-route, Suffolk Police conducted a search of the scene which revealed a button, similar to those attached to RAF greatcoats, lying near the corpse. Assisted by the knowledge that the RAF Corporal, on being discovered in the WAAF billet area, had informed the WAAF who challenged him that he was looking for the "Number One" billet, Police centred their attention on this site. It didn't, however, prevent them from questioning Italian prisoners and all new arrivals of RAF personnel who had been posted recently. This led to a certain amount of paranoia on the station, particularly to some unfortunate airmen who became murder

Taken on 16th October 1945, these two aerial photographs combine to show the majority of the RAF Beccles airfield. Aircraft parked on the loop dispersals around the perimeter include many Warwicks and an Anson (left page), while Sea Otters and Walruses surround the T2 hangar once occupied by British International Helicopters Ltd (right page). The Control Tower and Signals Square sit to the right of the lane running from the bottom of the left page diagonally across the airfield, which later became the Beccles to Hulver road.

Crown Copyright/MoD. Reproduced with the permission of the Controller of HMSO.

suspects on the first day at their new posting! All sorts of excuses arose for the type of events which, at any other time, would have scarcely attracted comment. A trail of blood leading to one airman's bed turned out to be from a rabbit he had caught, while another had to explain away scratches on his face when he had parted company with his bicycle and landed in a prickly bush. Eventually, Heys was singled out when the WAAF witness from the previous night identified him during the pay parade for the Number One site personnel. Being interviewed at Beccles Police station, wearing his RAF greatcoat with missing button, Heys was unaware of how much evidence against him had been accumulated. Admitting the episode at the WAAF site, but denying witness reports that he arrived at his billet during the early hours of Thursday or that he had risen before his companions to clean his uniform and shoes, Heys was released due to lack of evidence. The Police had no doubts, however, about his guilt. Forensic tests revealed traces of brick dust on Heys' shoes similar to those discovered on Winifred Evans' shoes, along with traces of blood on his tunic and a hair which had very likely been the dead woman's. Heys was arrested at Beccles Police station on Tuesday 5th December and charged with the murder of Winifred Evans. Committal proceedings at Beccles, following a bleak Christmas spent in Norwich prison, resulted in Heys being committed for trial at Bury St Edmunds on 19th January 1945. The police had spent their time well, interviewing everyone who had been close to him in his past service life. This revealed a Jekyll and Hyde character, a model husband and father when sober but becoming violent when drunk. The day the committal proceedings ended, a twist in the case occurred that sealed Arthur Heys' fate. A letter to his Commanding Officer, "confessing" to the murder and absolving Heys from any involvement, was handed in at Beccles police station. It contained sufficient detail of the known events of that terrible night for police to be left in no doubt that the letter had originated from Heys. Having established that it was possible for inmates to have letters smuggled out of Norwich prison, the police employed a Scotland Yard fingerprint expert, who had knowledge of handwriting analysis, to confirm that the letter was indeed from Heys' own hand. Any defence he might have had planned for the three day trial at Bury quickly evaporated when the letter was produced as evidence for the prosecution, but even so it failed to alter the accused's calm demeanour throughout. The outcome, thanks to the letter, was never in doubt and the jury took a mere forty minutes to return a guilty verdict, Heys protesting his innocence to the end. On Tuesday 13th March, 1945, Arthur Heys was executed at Norwich prison, the first hanging to take place there since 1938. Interest in the case appeared short lived, and with the struggle for Europe entering the final phase the personnel at RAF Beccles were too occupied elsewhere to dwell on the subject for very long. The daylight and night bombing of occupied Europe and Germany carried on unabated throughout the winter months, and brought a grim determination to the Air Sea Rescue organisation to provide as much support as they could to the bomber and fighter crews engaged on the final stages of the campaign.

CHAPTER 5

"WE SHALL BE THERE"
(280 Sqn Motto)

December 1944 to April 1945

December arrived with a drama for 280 Sqn, when on the 1st of the month Warrant Officer Tommy Pike's Warwick suffered an engine fire whilst on a local area "familiarisation" flight. Fortunately for all on board, the fire was extinguished quickly and the aircraft landed shortly after without further incident. The same crew were airborne again the following day, when three Warwicks were despatched from Beccles to search for a downed bomber crew in the area of Borkum and Helgoland, close to the German coast. On the 15th of the month Warwicks "S" and "U", the latter equipped with a lifeboat, were scrambled to locate and assist in the rescue of a ditched Fortress crew, who were eventually picked up by Royal Navy Rescue Motor Launch 523. Bad luck struck at Tommy Pike's crew again on 18th December, when a serious oil leak forced them to make an emergency landing at RAF Langham, 280 Sqn's former home. To cap an already eventful month, Christmas Eve saw the hapless crew return to Beccles on one engine after a six hour search. Gus Platts, a member of Tommy Pike's crew, and imbued with the customary superstition of an aviator, didn't believe in bad luck but did believe in good luck. Renowned for going on operations wearing a silk stocking round his neck that his wife gave to him following their first date, he was always asked by his "skipper" if he had it on after venturing aloft without it one night. Tommy Pike's crew had never been the same after an earlier incident, when the navigator brought an ivory elephant on board attached to a necklace, which the mid upper gunner took an instant dislike to as an omen of bad luck. Ignoring the warning, the navigator kept the offending "charm" on, causing an almighty row. During the subsequent flight, everything seemed to go wrong, with loud bangs from one of the engines accompanied by clouds of smoke, radio and radar going dead, and driving rain into the bargain. After all the crew had unsuccessfully begged the navigator to dispose of the "jinxed" elephant, the mid-upper gunner took matters into his own hands and, grabbing the elephant off it's chain, hurled it into the night. Soon the engine picked up again, the rain stopped and the flight ended uneventfully. Despite the crews conviction that the elephant had been "jinxed", the navigator didn't speak to the gunner for days afterwards.

Christmas Eve saw the arrival of American bombers and fighters, diverted due to fog and freezing conditions over much of Eastern England. These conditions had prevented large scale operations over the previous five days, and a maximum effort by the Eighth Air Force was required to support the beleaguered allied forces following the surprise German offensive in the Ardennes, later to be known as the "Battle of the Bulge", by attacking airfields and communications to the German front lines. This proved to be the largest air strike of the war, involving 2,046 heavy bombers and 853 fighter escorts, and constituted virtually every serviceable aircraft in the effort. Christmas gave a brief respite from operations, which all at RAF Beccles made the most of. Christmas dinner in the Airmen's Mess was, in the traditional way, served by the officers. Following on from this, the officers visited the Sergeants Mess for drinks, before returning to their own Mess for turkey and Christmas pudding, washed down with ample supplies of brandy and wine. Sleeping off the lunchtime excesses in the mess armchairs, there followed another session in the bar and a party to round off the proceedings. The mess was considered by the officers "very comfortable", equipped with a snooker table, piano and well stocked bar. It was usual during normal mess nights for the male officers to sing 'Goodnight, Ladies', at around 10.30 p.m., which acted as a signal for the many WAAF officers to depart. There followed a raucous sing-song of dirty RAF songs, which tended to be based on rugby songs, until a late hour. The station had, by this time, established their own entertainment in the form of a resident band and personnel took to the stage on 27th and 28th to perform a variety show and pantomime at the Public Hall for the benefit of the St John's Ambulance Brigade.

Operations resumed after Christmas, with a search for a dinghy by

"Party time" at RAF Beccles. Parties were held regularly to relieve boredom and allow the crews to "let off steam" in the confines of their Mess.

Warwick "B" of 280 Sqn on the 28th. On this occasion, the dinghy was found with the assistance of two circling Beaufighters. Within 20 miles of the Humber estuary, a rescue was effected by an RAF High Speed Launch and Royal Navy destroyer.

For a short period during December, RAF Beccles was the home for the servicing echelon of 612 Sqn, flying another Vickers type, the Wellington Mk.XIV.

New Year commenced with a hectic day for 280 Sqn, when on the 1st Warwick 'B' was scrambled to search for the crew of a downed Fortress of the 398th Bomb Group, USAAF, based at Nuthampstead, Hertfordshire. The aircraft was part of a general effort to disrupt German army communication lines and vital oil supplies necessary to sustain the counter-offensive in the Ardennes. Forced to abandon their fully laden bomber, which sank within 10 seconds of ditching, the six surviving crew were spotted in three dinghies by escorting Thunderbolts in a position 95 miles NE of Texel, Holland. Escorted by three Mustangs, the first Warwick was later joined by a second to assist in the search, then a third. This last Warwick, coded 'U', dropped it's cargo of Lindholme gear, only to see the parachutes fail to deploy. Joined by it's companions, the same fate occurred when 'A' dropped it's boat to be smashed into splinters on contact with the sea. Launching the boat was very similar to carrying out a bombing run, with some notable differences. After dropping smoke floats to indicate wind velocity, the Warwick would run in at 700' to 750', with the navigator spread-eagled in the nose over the plexiglass panel, switch-cord in hand to activate the lifeboat release mechanism. Giving final instructions to the pilot to adjust the aircraft's heading, the cry of "Boat Away" would be accompanied by a slight but noticeable lifting of the aircraft, unburdened of it's heavy and unwieldy load. Honours were left to the original aircraft despatched to execute a perfect boat drop from 700', which the grateful survivors were seen to board. From the initial scramble, the rescue had so far taken four and a half hours, and in the gathering darkness yet another Warwick, coded 'T', arrived to maintain contact with the lifeboat. After another two hours orbiting the spot, flares were dropped to guide a Navy 'B' Class Fairmile Motor Launch, based at Great Yarmouth, to complete the rescue.

The following day, Warwicks 'A' and 'K', the former with lifeboat underslung, were despatched from Beccles, again with an escort of Mustangs, to conduct a search. Fifty miles west of Helgoland, and with the aid of an automatic homing signal, a stationary lifeboat was located carrying four aircrew, closely accompanied by a floating mine. Dropping it's lifeboat to provide either fuel for the other boat or an alternative means of escape, the crew of Warwick 'A' were surprised to receive no acknowledgement from the survivors, nor notice any action taken to go alongside the newly arrived lifeboat. Before departing the scene, 'K' dropped it's Lindholme gear as an additional aid. On the 3rd January, the downed crew were located after drifting westwards from their original position, and were dropped another boat from Warwick 'X'. Again no attempt was made to reach this boat, so fuel canisters were dropped separately, on this occasion being retrieved by the downed crew. The next day, searches failed to locate the boat until darkness fell and, aware that motor launches were in the area, Warwick 'K' dropped flares over the still stationary boat until the launches arrived.

Not all 280 Squadron's duties ended in rescues. Gus Platts recalled a story which, though by no means typical, embodies the frustration felt by many of the Warwick crews when they were unable to assist a stricken aircraft.

"It was a daylight job, and we flew with the USAAF on their bombing missions. Not all the way, unfortunately, because while we were in the middle of them we felt secure. Their huge formations used to take ages to form, so we used to wait till they were clear of the coast before catching them up and slotting into the formation. Dropping out of formation near the enemy coast, we would monitor their radio messages which started on arrival over the target, when all hell broke loose. The raid returned, trying to maintain it's neat formation. We watched and listened for those who couldn't keep up, those with engines out, trailing smoke, or throttled back so the wings didn't fold up or the elevators tear off. Bomb doors open, the wheels sometimes down, some flying with a distinct yaw or one wing low. Many had 'bought it' over the target, and those we would never see. We were only interested in the stragglers, particularly those that didn't look like they would make it to the East Anglian coast. These came in all shapes and sizes, and we soon learned to judge their troubles. Injured pilots, dead navigators, gun turrets shattered, they would be easy pickings for the Luftwaffe. Here's where we came into our own, with our first class navigators, fresh firepower and, most of all, our morale-boosting value. The American crews knew that if they could only make the sea, a lifeboat would be dropped, their position reported and orbited until more help arrived. At times we would fly alongside those heading in completely the wrong direction to reach land, waggling our wings and trying to head them in the right direction. Adjusting our speed to theirs, we would be gratified to see grinning faces, friendly recognition and the occasional rude signs from behind perspex windows and blisters. We were 'Big Brother' and 'Little Friend', and often the only RAF roundels the American crews had ever formed up with.

Then came the day we picked up a Liberator all on it's own, with one propeller fully feathered, and slightly off course. We flew up and waggled our wings for attention. Some of their aircraft recognition wasn't too good so we always crept up to them. There were no smiling faces, no rude signs.

Not a thing except someone sitting in the pilot's seat looking straight ahead. There was no co-pilot, no gunners, no-one in the astrodome. She was a clean ship, in very good condition. There was no apparent damage, no oil leaks, nor any holes in her. Everyone in the crew got a weird sensation as we flew around her searching for her problem. After viewing her from below, we climbed to her port quarter. Though the pilot carried on looking forward, the Liberator adjusted it's course to ours. As we flew across the North Sea, all attempts to contact the bomber with Aldis lamp and radio proved fruitless. From somewhere behind there was another 'Mayday' called, but we couldn't deal with it. Then on the far horizon the grey sea became a different shade and a coastline started to form. We were making landfall close to Cromer. For the first time something happened on the Liberator. A voice called over the radio, "I can see the coast now. You can leave me." No please or thank you, nor friendly cuss words, nor explanation. There was still the other 'Mayday' and Tommy Pike swung the Warwick round and opened the throttles wide. We couldn't find the other aircraft. He had probably gone down in 'the drink', but we didn't look for long as we got a report from the Cromer lifeboat that we were no sooner out of sight when our Liberator started to lose altitude, ditching into the sea about 8 miles off Cromer. The Cromer lifeboat had put out to sea, and we returned to the scene, but there was no sign of wreckage, bodies, or dinghies. All that greeted us was a very slow rolling, calm swell that had closed over what we always remembered as our Mary Celeste."

After dark on the 3rd January, the area around the airfield was rocked by a huge explosion, when a V-1 flying bomb, or "Doodlebug" as they were commonly referred to, came down in a field in the Ellough area, having been hit by anti-aircraft fire. The explosion from 847 kgs of various explosives contained within the V-1 resulted in a 24 ft wide crater approximately ? mile WSW of All Saints Church, Ellough, breaking a flagstaff and 13 windows. Numbers 1-6, Rectory Cottages also suffered broken windows, as did a further seven dwellings in the area. Thankfully, there were no casualties from this incident.

On 17th January, Andy Padbury's crew were detailed to accompany a squadron of RAF Wellingtons to provide a radio link for relaying important information back. The bombers were going in very low to attack German convoys off the Dutch coast, and would not have sufficient height to make contact with the UK. The information was passed to the Warwick by radio, then transmitted in Morse code. Alone at 10,000', the Warwick crew were conscious of their exposed position, as the transmissions were quickly picked up by German direction finding stations that were in direct communication with patrolling enemy night fighters. Dodging searchlights, flying in and out of clouds, and aided by the blackness of the night, they made it safely home to Beccles.

Station life took on a routine look, with orders being issued that 'Gum boots' were not to be worn as a matter of convenience, but only when strictly necessary, and instructions that on no account should farmer's fields be used as short cuts between the widely dispersed accommodation. It was hardly surprising that the crews took to wearing whatever was available to keep warm and dry. The cold, damp accommodation, remote from the hangers and aircraft, was made worse by the terrible winter weather. Persistent fog, long periods of severe freezing conditions, alternating with thaws and then more snow and ice all combined to stretch personnel to their limits.

If the ground crews had a miserable time, the aircrew did their best to keep their spirits up. The crews of 280 Sqn spent their spare time pursuing a variety of pastimes, besides frequenting the increasingly popular haunts of the "Black Boy", "Bear and Bells" and the "Fleece" in nearby Beccles, which always seemed blessed with ample quantities of beer. On the station, shooting was popular, with crew competitions for target shooting, usually for a nominal "prize" that was exceeded by the drinks bill in the bar afterwards. Sometimes the crews would compete with local farmers in clay shoots, where the Air Gunners deflection shooting no doubt came in for some close scrutiny. The station medical officer cultivated community relations in his own way, building a rapport with the matron and nurses at the town's cottage hospital. Returning the visits on regularly held party nights, the nurses were entertained by the station's band.

Returning to operations, Warwick 'U' came to grief on landing back at Beccles on 29th January, the starboard wing catching fire and burning off, fortunately without injury to the crew. Five days later Warwick 'Z', flown by Flight Lieutenant Radford, was diverted from her patrol line to a position 50 miles WNW of Den Helder, where a Fortress returning from a Berlin raid had been spotted flying perilously close to the sea. Guided by a pair of circling Thunderbolts, two aircrew were spotted in a dinghy, marked by another 280 Sqn Warwick, 'O', dropping smoke floats. A boat was successfully deposited at the scene by 'Z', just prior to RAF High Speed Launch 2631 appearing over the horizon. Boarding the vessel direct from the dinghy, the lifeboat was sunk by gunfire to avoid initiating another rescue operation. Diverted to another reported ditching, the Warwick duo were rewarded with a sighting of three dinghies containing seven survivors, thirty miles west of the Dutch island of Texel. Dropping a set of Lindholme gear, 'Z' called for assistance and orbited until a Catalina flying boat arrived to evacuate the dinghy occupants.

February arrived, and with it V2 rockets to add to the hazards of flying close to the enemy held coast. On one occasion, Andy Padbury's crew found themselves directly over a launch site when a V2 rose from the ground, passing within a few yards of the Warwick. Having recovered the aircraft to an even keel after being caught in the slipstream, the pilot let fly a string of expletives, asking "what the !!!! had caused that?" Though few of the airmen stationed at Beccles saw a V2 that close, some were only too grateful to return after leave, having seen first hand the results of Hitler's latest "Revenge" weapon on their home towns and cities.

On 14th of the month Flight Lieutenant W.B. Thompson, flying Warwick "N", took off at 8:25 am on a routine patrol. At 3:55 pm, still on patrol, he called RAF Beccles control for instructions, and received the response 8 minutes later to return to base. Though 8 minutes may not have seemed like a long time, in terms of fuel burn at the end of a long mission, it proved decisive. At 4:42 pm, just short of the duty runway and on the Mutford side of the airfield, the aircrafts tanks were dry and it ploughed into a field, fortunately without serious injury to the crew. Local youngsters were soon on the scene, and salvaged, amongst other things, plexiglass from the canopy which they turned into jewelry to supplement their pocket money. The aircraft was dismantled and removed for repair shortly afterwards. The following day a B-24 Liberator of the 446th Bomb Group, the "Bungay Buckaroos" from Flixton, crash landed with battle damage following a raid on synthetic oil installations at Magdeburg by 372 B-24's. The target had been hit through 9/10 cloud using H2X equipment.

RAF Beccles became "terra firma" for yet another American heavy bomber when, on the 23rd of the month, B-24H Liberator serial number 42-50319, from the 445th Bomb Group at Tibenham, Norfolk, made an emergency landing with the inner port engine feathered. On this occasion, the target of the 368 B-24's dispatched was the German road and rail communication network, part of a major assault codenamed "Operation Clarion".

On 26th February, two venerable Supermarine Walrus MkII's arrived at RAF Beccles to supplement the Air Sea Rescue services with their amphibious capability. Along with their five crews, the numbers eventually grew to six aircraft, constituting "C" flight of 278 Squadron, under the command of Flight Lieutenant Robertson. The Squadron had been formed in October 1941 at Matlaske, Norfolk, specifically to fulfill the Air Sea Rescue role around East Anglia, a role which eventually incorporated the South-East coast. The remainder of 278 Sqn was split between Thorney Island, Hampshire, and Hawkinge, Kent. The poorly armed Walruses, though slow and with a limited range, were very manoeuvrable and could put down in heavy seas. Of course, taking off again was another matter, and on many occasions the sturdy wooden-hulled biplanes were forced to taxi back to the nearest port, escorted by navy gunboats.

Tragedy was to strike 278 Sqn early in March, when on the 6th Flight Lieutenants Robertson and Walker, accompanied by Warrant Officer

Leonard Carpenter, took Walrus "S" into the air for a search off the Humberside coast. At 10:55 am, in a position off Flamborough Head, the aircraft was observed to crash into the sea and break up, taking all on board to a watery grave and leaving only a small amount of oil and some wreckage for the Seagull amphibians that arrived soon after. March continued in sombre mood for 278 Sqn, when Walrus P5663 landed 15 miles NE of Great Yarmouth to recover the dead body of a Spitfire pilot, only to have to taxi into Gorleston because of the heavy sea running. The prospect of ditching in a fighter aircraft was viewed with dread by most pilots, and with a survival time in the freezing waters of the North Sea of between 5 and 10 minutes during the winter months, their only hope was to get into the aircraft's dinghy as quickly as possible and hope that the last radio call made gave an accurate "fix" for the search aircraft and boats.

For the Warwicks of 280 Sqn, March proved their busiest month in terms of hours flown, though things didn't really "liven up" until the end of the month. On the 24th, 280 Sqn provided cover for the massive air armada of tugs, gliders, bombers and fighters that were engaged in the airborne landings on the Rhine. The sight of thousands of aircraft passing overhead impressed the crews, even though vast numbers were commonplace during the daylight bombing campaign by the allies. Fortunately, there were few "customers", and the Luftwaffe was too busy elsewhere to interfere with the lonely Warwicks. Two days later, Andy Padbury's crew were diverted to RAF Langham, Norfolk, due to thick fog at Beccles, where there were some Fortresses residing. Hearing that a Fortress was coming in with two engines on fire, the Warwick crew decamped from the Mess to watch the proceedings. After executing a wheels-up landing on the grass beside the runway, the heavily damaged aircraft slewed towards the Mess. The RAF crew scattered in all directions, and were relieved to see the Fortress come to a standstill in a hedge a few yards from the Mess.

The members of 280 Sqn were by no means safer in the air, as an incident during the month proved. The Luftwaffe, though very much on the defensive, was still occasionally in evidence, as Gus Platts recalled.

'Laying in bed but not yet asleep, I heard a Warwick pass low overhead. "Queffers," I said to my wife. "His crew are due back about now." A few seconds later, I heard the roar of another aircraft on his tail, followed by machine gun and cannon fire, then silence. Two weeks prior to that, we had been warned to land with our turrets manned, as "Jerry" had started following our aircraft back. Waiting until just before landing to strike, they knew we would be at our most vulnerable, with guns secured for landing. This time the turret was manned by a very alert gunner, and no one was shot down.....on either side.' The enemy activity in the area wasn't confined to attacks on aircraft, as one of the last German intruder raids of the war resulted in excess of fifty small SD10 anti-personnel bombs arriving in the southern area of Beccles on 4th March. No-one was injured and it was rumoured that the intended target was the mobile beacon which guided aircraft back to the airfield.

On the last day of March, a rescue began which would sap the resources of not just 280 Sqn, but most of the other Air Sea Rescue services in the local area.

The story begins on the 30th March, during an American daylight raid. Flying top cover for the raid, a P-51 Mustang belonging to the 363rd Fighter Squadron of the high scoring 357th Fighter Group, based at Leiston, Suffolk, was forced to leave formation off the island of Borkum, owing to the cooling system choking up. The pilot, Don Myers, knew the Mustang couldn't carry out a successful ditching because of the large intake on the underside of the aircraft, which would act as a scoop when it made contact with the water. Choosing instead to bail out, his parachute was seen by other Mustangs of the group, who orbited the position while they waited for help to arrive. The response came initially from another American unit, the 5th Emergency Rescue Squadron, which was based at RAF Halesworth, Suffolk. Equipped with a mixture of P-47 Thunderbolts, lifeboat-equipped B-17 Flying Fortresses, and Consolidated OA-10A Catalina flying boats, it was to be one of the latter which was despatched first to the scene. Escorted by three Mustangs of the 357th, the "Cat" was forced to make an emergency landing in the sea about 15 miles NE of Juist after developing engine trouble.

The following day, Warwicks were scrambled from RAF Beccles, escorted by American P-51 Mustangs from the 357th Fighter Group, to search for the downed Catalina. Meanwhile "Teamwork 75", another Catalina from Halesworth, had been despatched to the area to assist in the search. Before reaching the scene, it was diverted to a new position where a sighting had been made of a survivor adrift in a dinghy. Locating the dinghy, the Catalina alighted on the rough sea, only to have it's Port engine damaged by a large wave crashing into it. It was now a question of survival for the Catalina crew, as contact had been lost with the dinghy they had landed to assist. The situation was becoming serious, with downed crews spread over a wide area adjacent to the enemy coastline. Air Sea Rescue resources were mobilised again on 1st April, and 280 Sqn provided their Warwicks to assist in the effort.

One of the Warwicks scrambled that day was Gus Platts', whose crew had a drama of their own to contend with during their patrol. Gus takes up the story....

'I was dividing my time between searching the sea for any signs of life and the air for any sign of sudden death, when suddenly the intercom erupted. "Christ! An aeroplane, coming like the clappers of Hell!"

The voice was Vince Keeley's, the mid-upper gunner. "Where? Call it out," retorted the skipper, Tommy. "It's coming like the clappers," came the reply. "Call it out. Where is it? Who is that?" None of us had any idea where

Supermarine Walrus ASR MkII flies low over a downed fighter pilot before making an attempt to land Imperial War Museum, Neg No.HU1760A)

the enemy aircraft was coming from. I searched the sky in every direction. The late sun was over the nose and the front gunner would be looking up there. We are talking about fractions of a second. Some instinct told me the attack would be out of the sun. I gambled and depressed the guns, half standing, braced, and looked below. If it had been a head-on or beam attack, we could have been in trouble. I could hear the mid-upper guns crackling and the enemy cannon, and suddenly there it was. He was so far below and going so fast I couldn't believe it. I hosed the air around him but my tracer seemed to be slower than he was, and he seemed to be leaving it behind. An optical illusion of course, but our apparent relative speed from which a gunner bases his calculations was about 875 mph! His fuselage seemed to be triangular in section, with low wings and two underslung round engines. His black silhouette sliced away towards his homeland without returning for a second attack. Whether he had a problem, or was hit by our bullets, we would never know. The skipper was very upset that he hadn't been able to take evasive action, saying any advice to weave either port or starboard would have been preferable to "like the clappers of Hell!" Back at Beccles, an inspection of the Warwick revealed not a scratch. At de-briefing, I drew the silhouette of the aircraft I saw. Vince said that it didn't have propellers. I drew the shape of a Messerschmitt Me262. "They are flying their jets," said the debriefing officer as he shook his head. "Now we are for it!"

It transpired that the Messerschmitt had tangled with the American Mustangs escorting the Catalina just prior to the Warwick incident, which may have accounted for the single firing pass made by the German jet. Major L.K. Carson was one of the Mustang pilots, and claimed a 'Probable' in the melee, and it was quite possible that the Me262 encountered by the Warwick was the same one. The incident did not prevent the Warwick from locating the downed Catalina and dropping a Lifeboat and Lindholme gear to the crew. Landing about 100 yards from the "Cat", the latter's pilot tried to taxy alongside the lifeboat using his remaining usable engine, only to damage the boat with the aircraft's tail in the heavy seas. By 1200 hrs, the Messerschmitts were back, strafing the hapless flying boat with cannon fire, severing the tail and further damaging the Port wing. As it settled low in the water, the crew took to dinghies, thankful to be uninjured in the latest episode of their ordeal. Gus Platts, now flying in Warwick 'Y' with Flying Officer Maxwell, returned to the scene late in the afternoon, accompanied by another two Warwicks from Beccles. Visibility had deteriorated, with overcast at 8,000' and haze up to about 4,000'. Nearing the scene, the seven escorting Mustangs turned back due to the weather, leaving the three Warwicks to cling to the wavetops for safety. Entering the bay, the dinghies were quickly located and the Warwicks prepared to drop their cargoes, aware of their own vulnerability in the proximity of the German anti-aircraft batteries. A lifeboat and Lindolme gear were successfully dropped, although when the downed crew reached the boat they were dismayed to find it damaged and taking water, necessitating their return to the dinghies. The Warwick crews fears were well founded for, as 'Y' circled the spot, it was suddenly bracketed by shell bursts. Gus Platts thought his number was up.

"I don't know what I was dreaming about, but suddenly the air around me was filled with Hell. It was like every gun in Germany and on every surrounding island fired on us at once. One second it was clear and peaceful and the next the sky erupted with a thousand bursts of flak and my turret became a birdcage without perspex. I could feel no pain. There was no blood splashing about anywhere but when you're legs are off they tell me that you can't feel it. I tried to look down at them as I fumbled for the mouthpiece of the intercom, which was hanging by it's wire from my neck. I could see my knees, they moved. I was trying to speak. My mouth moved, my jaw moved, my lips moved. The switch was 'On' but no sound came. Fabric trailed back from the tail, along with pieces of metal. 'Climb, Dive, Corkscrew'. I do not know what everyone was calling but they were all, apart from me, yelling something as Maxwell tried to control the aircraft in the vicious air. I tried to look round at the rudder, and saw that it too was damaged. 'Skipper' came from my mouth at last. 'Tail Gunner here. Take it VERY easy, we've been hit. Damage to our elevators and rudder. Go very slowly down to the deck. Very slowly.' We eased back down to sea level and Maxwell circled back towards England, cutting the throttles and keeping his fingers crossed. The turret still worked, and I fired a burst to make sure the guns still worked, but it was a very drafty birdcage as I sat and felt for any damage to my body. We landed at Beccles and by now I was calm of course, but I had not counted on the impression I had made. 'God, you were so cool, Gus' someone said. 'Everyone panicked except you,' and then Flying Officer Maxwell added 'You were great. I couldn't see the flak from up front but I could sure feel it. I like the way you waited for everyone to stop yelling, and then your voice came in so quiet and confident. It had a calming effect on everyone. That,s the advantage of your past experience.' I just had to tell them the truth, and I did."

Following the Warwicks out had been a lifeboat equipped B-17 Flying Fortress, codenamed 'Teamwork 88'. This aircraft made the first operational drop of an American A-1 airborne lifeboat, which landed 200 yards from the dinghies and into which the grateful survivors boarded. They managed to get the boat under way, and headed at 5 knots towards England, on a course marked by smoke floats from one of 280's Warwicks. The continuing poor visibility and low cloud base kept all the search aircraft on the ground the next day, and it wasn't till the 3rd April that the Warwicks from Beccles sighted the lifeboat, now dead in the water in a position 50 miles NW of Borkum. The engine had stopped, and the survivors were in poor condition from the continual soakings and bitter cold. Warwick 'K' was the first to make contact, picking up and homing onto an S.O.S. radio signal emitted from the boat. Another boat and some spare petrol cans were dropped by 'K', but the weary survivors were too weak to reach the boat. Retrieving the petrol cans from the sea, they attempted to start the engines of their own boat, which by now had become salt contaminated from the heavy sea running. Later in the day Warwick 'E' dropped the fifth lifeboat used during the rescue, but again tiredness and exposure combined to prevent the downed crew reaching it. The Navy arrived on the scene, in the shape of a unit of 'Z' Class Rescue Launches from H.M.S. Midge at Great Yarmouth, operating at the limit of their range. In darkness the Warwick dropped a series of flares to guide the Navy vessels to within sighting distance, which was very limited due to the black night and heavy seas. The search was temporarily suspended, the vessels cutting their engines and resuming at daybreak. All the while Warwicks maintained their vigil over the lifeboat, dropping flares despite their proximity to the enemy coastline. The lifeboat was finally located and the survivors taken aboard the Navy vessels, cold, wet, but grateful. The six lives saved had taken up the resources of a large element of the Air Sea Rescue Services, been carried out extremely close to the enemy coast, in appalling conditions, and in airspace threatened by one of the latest and fastest German jet fighters in service. The successful outcome is testimony to the unstinting efforts of all the personnel involved.

CHAPTER 6

"Like a Thunderbolt from Heaven"
(Motto, 810 Sqn, FAA)

April to May 1945

On 9th April a second Fleet Air Arm unit to be stationed at RAF Beccles during the war years arrived for an eventful stay. Based at RAF Thorney Island, near Portsmouth, 810 Sqn were employed on anti-submarine patrols off the coast of Northern France. As the allied armies moved North into Belgium and the Germans were denied more and more ports, the requirement for anti-submarine patrols moved North and Eastwards, out of range of the south coast airfields. The move came suddenly for the crews of 810 Sqn, who had settled into their comfortable quarters in the RAF station. Victor Lease, a member of 810, was on 48 hour leave in Dulwich. Arriving home after a date with his girlfriend on the evening of the 8th April, he found a message to ring the Duty Officer at Thorney Island. He was told to rejoin the squadron as soon as possible as it was leaving the next morning. Dashing to Waterloo Station, he boarded a mail train just before 3 am on the 9th, arriving at Havant at 6 am. Packing his kit and taking breakfast in the mess, he discovered the next posting was RAF Beccles, but as his normal pilot was still in the Midlands, he was forced to make the journey in another Barracuda. Arrival at Beccles was made mid afternoon, the ugly Barracudas arriving in two line astern formations. The crews quickly disembarked, to be treated by their Commanding Officer to the first round of half-pints in their new mess. The ground crews had a more arduous journey, arriving by road with all their kit and spares for the aircraft.

The squadron had re-equipped in February 1945 with the Fairey Barracuda Mk III - known in Fleet Air Arm parlance as the "Pregnant Barra", because of the radome under the fuselage which housed the fully rotatable scanner of the ASV Mk 10 radar (Air to Surface Vessel). Armed with under-wing depth charges and machine guns for defence, the earlier marks of Barracuda had performed sterling work in the attacks on the Tirpitz in Norway, the oil installations on Sumatra and in support of the allied amphibious landings at Salerno in Italy. The aircraft was of unusual design, being a large, heavy, shoulder-wing all metal monoplane. The aerodynamic effect of it's large rectangular flaps mounted inboard of the ailerons led to a high-set braced tailplane instead of the usual position mounted at the base of the tail fin. The Barracuda carried a crew of three - pilot, observer/navigator and wireless operator/gunner. Initial inexperience of operating such a heavy aircraft resulted in many accidents, owing to the crew's former mounts being Swordfish and Albacore biplanes. The latter had the ability to glide down following engine failure, a feature not shared by the Barracuda. Crews for 810 were seconded from other units and the squadron worked up in rapid time to take on anti-submarine and anti-shipping patrols round the Channel Isles. Moving to RAF Beccles, the Barracudas were tasked with several roles, the primary one being Anti-Small-Battle-Unit Patrols. This requirement came about from the growing menace of German mini-submarines, which were causing problems to allied shipping operating in the area of the Schelde Estuary off Antwerp. The midget subs had first appeared during the Normandy landings in 1944, and had accounted for several allied vessels, though at considerable cost to themselves. One of two main types encountered was the "Biber", a 30' long, 6.5 ton beast, petrol driven and with a top speed of 6.5 knots on the surface and 5.3 knots submerged. With a range of 130 miles surface and only 8.6 miles submerged, the mine-equipped Bibers were easy prey for any patrolling allied aircraft. The crew were hardly encouraged to submerge the vessel in any case, since it was unstable under water, couldn't maintain a standard depth, and was more than likely to poison them with carbon monoxide from the exhaust. The second type was the "Seehund", a larger midget submarine developed with the benefit of technology gained from the capture of British "X" craft after an attack on the Tirpitz. With a surface range of 120 miles at 8 knots and 20 miles at 3 knots submerged, and weighing 7 tons, the two-man Seehunds were armed with twin torpedos slung either side of the keel. The plan for 810 Sqn was to maintain a patrol line during daylight hours some miles off the Dutch Coast and right across the mouth of the Schelde. Operating alongside the Warwicks of 280 Sqn, there was also a good opportunity to obtain some "spotting" assistance from them while they carried out their long patrols in the area. A fully fuelled and armed Barracuda was always on readiness at Beccles to "scramble", should a sighting be reported. Owing to limitations on the Barracuda's range, and allowing six 250 lb depth charges to be carried, all "non-essential" equipment was dispensed with including, much to the crew's consternation, the twin Vickers machine guns which were their only defence. Patrolling at 120 knots at a height of 800', the Barracudas were a tempting target for German jet and rocket fighters known to frequent the area. Protection was therefore provided in the shape of five powerful twin-engined Bristol Beaufighters, which although could not carry out close escort, were always in the area. Using the 3 cm radar on board the Barracudas, standard practice was to turn away from any unidentified "blips" appearing on the screen until the potential threat had departed the scene. Fortunately, one crew discovered the presence of an enemy fighter just in time, for having already identified it as a P-47 Thunderbolt, were dismayed to find out it was a Focke Wulf 190, heading straight for them. They only got away due to the prescence of a sea mist, which afforded them enough cover to make their escape.

Another task to befall 810 Sqn was to patrol the East Coast shipping lanes from the Thames Estuary to the Wash. This was only carried out when the British "X" craft weren't exercising in their designated training area off Lowestoft. The sorties lasted mostly three to four hours, with the crews rotating duties to cover the daylight hours. Because of the duty rota and the wide dispersal of sites at RAF Beccles, many of the crews didn't see much of each other during the period of their stay. Bacon, egg and chips were provided before and after each sortie, to ensure the crews had a protein filled meal to keep them going longer in the event they were forced to ditch in the sea. One of the most dangerous elements of the sorties was the return over the Suffolk coast. There existed a two mile wide "gate" over Southwold, through which the Barracudas were to fly, at a given height and perpendicular to the shore. As an added identifying method, a series of flares had to be fired off in the correct order. For example, between 1200 and 1600 hour the code sequence would be red, red, green, changing for the following four hours to white, green, red, and so on throughout the 24 hours of the day. The crews hoped that the Army gunners were using the same codes, as they were known to shoot first and ask questions afterwards. To get back to the airfield in the hours of darkness, the aircraft had to overfly a mobile beacon which transmitted two identity letters, again changing codes every four hours. To add to the secrecy, the beacon's position was moved every day or so. This was designed to avert German night fighters following allied aircraft back to their bases.

Offensive operations commenced on 10th April, after a Warwick spotted an enemy midget sub. One of two Sub Lieutenant McCarthy's in the squadron was despatched to attack the vessel with an escort of three Thunderbolts. Dropping four depth charges, the "Biber" escaped unharmed after the embarrassed Barracuda crew realised that the fuses hadn't been set. Over the next two days further sightings resulted in two more attacks being made on "Bibers". One was abandoned on the surface after a depth charge attack, to be later towed into Great Yarmouth. A second received a near miss the following day after an attack by Petty Officer Tyler's Barracuda approximately 30 miles east of Lowestoft, although the only hint of damage found was some oil left on the surface of the sea. On 13th April Barracuda "L" found a "Seehund" running on the surface. Attempting to crash-dive, the sub was attacked from 200', the four depth charges exploding alongside. Set to explode at a depth of 25', the resulting explosions caused the Barracuda to lose sight of the sub. However, two survivors, one of whom appeared wounded, rose to the surface, and were seen to swim to a dinghy dropped by the attacking aircraft. A member of 810 Sqn at the time, James Moorhouse, remembered walking on the airfield when the Barracuda returned, and seeing it "beat up" the airfield in celebration. On the same day, Sub Lieutenant Bradbury claimed a "probable" following an attack on yet another mini-sub off the Dutch coast.

While 810 Sqn were kept busy with midget subs, the Warwicks of 280 continued their rescue sorties far out over the North Sea. On the 10th April, Warwick 'T', flown by Flight Lieutenant Radford and escorted by P-47 Thunderbolts, was despatched to locate two fighter pilots who had ditched off the Dutch coast. Just off Den Helder the first was located and a successful lifeboat drop made to him. Having boarded the boat, the enemy gun emplacements ashore decided to join in the proceedings and opened up on the unfortunate airman, by now struggling unsuccessfully to start the unfamiliar lifeboat engines. Orbiting the scene, the Warwick located a second dinghy and it's charge close by, and dropped his remaining Lindholme gear. With the aid of an offshore breeze, both dinghy and lifeboat were carried away from the coast and out of range of the guns. The Warwick continued to circle the scene until a couple of hours later, when an American Catalina alighted nearby to take the two grateful survivors aboard.

On the 18th of the month a less happy result was achieved by Flight Lieutenant Radford and Warrant Officer Tommy Pike's crews. Patrolling off the Frisian Islands, a column of smoke was spotted NE of Borkum,

810 Squadron's ungainly Fairey Barracuda MkIII's made an unusual sight in the skies over Beccles during their posting on Anti-Small Battle Unit Patrols off the Schelde Estuary. The radome housing on the underside of the rear fuselage led to the nickname the "Pregnant Barra" (Imperial War Museum, Neg No.MH6269)

marking the location of seven men in the water. Warwick 'P' dropped it's boat close to two men, while Warwick 'Y' discharged hers to another group of five. Weakened by the freezing water, the men's pathetic attempts to board the boats could only be watched with pity from above. Dropping further Mae Wests and dinghies, Walruses and Catalinas were requested while Warwick 'B' arrived on the scene as relief, but by 1700 hours it was apparent that all the men were dead. The same day Warwick 'T' was in the Borkum area and found a man in the water further out to sea than the larger group and dropped it's boat, followed by two sets of Linholme gear. All received no response from below. A Catalina arrived later and picked up three bodies, all that signalled the end of Handley Page Halifax 'L' of 420 (Snowy Owl) Sqn, Royal Canadian Air Force, based at RAF Tholthorpe, North Yorkshire.

Both the RAF and the USAAF didn't let up on the bombing campaign of the enemy homeland, and a large USAAF raid on the 17th of the month led to the last American crash landing of the war at Beccles when a P-51 Mustang of the 364th Fighter Group from Honington in Suffolk arrived, having run out of fuel escorting a heavy bomber raid on rail targets in SE Germany and Czechoslovakia. The group had engaged Me262 jet fighters during the mission, both in the air and on their airfields.

Damaged aircraft weren't the only hazard to "touch down" at RAF Beccles, as Sub Lieutenant McCarthy proved on 22nd April. Landing on the duty runway after a patrol, four depth charges were dropped causing some consternation on the station but thankfully without going off. The incident was recorded in the Squadron Log as "putting up a large black", which no doubt led to a considerable amount of leg-pulling and several rounds in the mess!

Unserviceability and bad weather in the form of snow, ice and fog caused problems during the month. On the 24th, Barracuda 'F' was determined to be unserviceable by the pilot through engine trouble. After a successful ground test, the aircraft was deemed serviceable and sent on a patrol off the Dutch coast, only for the pilot to carry out a crash landing at Nieuport in Belgium due to a recurrence of the earlier problem. Five days later, winds of up to 50 knots caused the diversion of a Warwick to Bradwell Bay, while another two and a Barracuda were diverted to RAF Manston in Kent. The pilot of the latter was Derek "Dusty" Rhodes, who recalled vividly the frightening sensation of landing in poor visibility with FIDO lit. This stood for "Fog, Intensive Dispersal Of", and consisted of a runway flanked by troughs flooded with fuel, which when lit, guided the aircraft down. Landing through it was described as the equivalent of a trip to Dante's Inferno, and not without hazard to the aircraft should they stray from the runway after touch down.

During the period social activities at RAF Beccles gathered pace as the sense of pending victory dawned. Bomber raids were gradually being succeeded by leaflet or food dropping and reconnaissance missions as the allies tightened the noose on the remainder of Hitler's dwindling armed forces. Plays became commonplace in the station's theatre, with Terence Rattigan's "Flare Path" being staged by a touring group from RAF Greyfriars, while the resident RAF "Beccles Follies" presented their own version of "Nuts in May", a concert party with a variety of exotic acts and songs from the time. A footnote to the programme clearly stated that "no fruit, flowers or vegetables were to be handed (or thrown) over the footlights" - instead they were to be sent to the Airmen's Mess. The show was such a success that it was later repeated in the Public Hall in Beccles. Some airmen, like Canadian Gus Platts, were fortunate enough to be allowed to live off camp with their wives, staying in local houses. Though rationing was common wherever you were, the warm front room, feather bed and indoor toilets were a welcome change from cold, damp nissen huts with their smoky stoves, outside toilets and showers, and the dubious pleasure of mess food. With a pub just around the corner, favourites for the aircrew proved to be the Black Boy in Ingate and the Horse and Groom at the bottom of Denmark Road. The Black Boy was particularly favoured by both RAF and FAA crews, mainly because it offered, in addition to the liquid refreshment, a chance to find out what was going on operationally, the latest flying programme, and what the future plans were. All this was carried out despite the constant entreaties by the powers that be regarding security and the need to restrict the flow of information to essential personnel only. Sometimes a visiting wife would give the crews a chance to eat out at a local hostelry. Steve Dawson remembered being invited to the Kings Head with his colleagues for a meal with the skippers wife. Unfortunately, the management were far from impressed when, later in the evening, the three Canadians in the crew were discovered playing dice in the entrance hallway. When the weather permitted, aircrew were allowed to "test" the lifeboats on the river Waveney, often accompanied by their wives and children and the occasional picnic. Alternatively, off duty periods could be spent shopping in Norwich or Great Yarmouth.

May started with the usual mix of weather, which hampered operations. Dusty Rhodes, embarking on the morning patrol in his Barracuda on the 6th, was warned that he may have to land away due to the worsening conditions. After groping his way to dispersal, he rang operations to point out the extent of the mist and low cloud that was by now blanketing the airfield, to be told quite calmly that it was "good enough". With a successful pre-flight check, Dusty carefully taxied the Barracuda to the end of the duty runway, when the Radio Operator reported the mission was cancelled just prior to the throttle being opened for take off. Instead the crew went on leave the following day and took the first train out of Beccles, much to the relief of Dusty, who was due to be married at Didsbury on the 8th. On arrival at Manchester railway station, the cries from the newspaper

Though very much the "Cinderella" of Coastal Command, the Air Sea Rescue Squadrons occasionally received some recognition. The variety of crew dress is evident in this picture of 280 Sqn members in front of their Warwick during the making of an RAF information film.

stands indicated that the war in Europe was at last over. Others based at Beccles were going in the other direction. Victor Lease, on leave in London, was aware of the impending announcement and saw the crowds thronging in Trafalgar Square that afternoon. With his leave expiring that night, he arrived back at the airfield to find a party to end all parties had already started, following Winston Churchill's announcement on the radio in the middle of the afternoon. Festivities extended late into the night, even though operations hadn't, as yet, been suspended. The jubilant station personnel were somewhat irked to find that all the pyrotechnics had been put safely under lock and key, but this didn't prevent somebody improvising by setting alight to a nearby hayrick. Although the war was officially over, the following day was the beginning of a slow winding down period for RAF Beccles, heralding an uncertain but as yet positive future.

CHAPTER 7
RETURN TO PEACE
VE Day to November 1945

Victor Lease had only been in bed a few hours, following the party the previous night, when he was roused by his steward at 0400 hrs for the dawn patrol. Pulling on sweater and battledress over his pyjamas, he made his way to the dispersal where Barracuda 'R' of 810 Sqn was parked. Taking off at 0440 hrs for the first patrol of VE Day, the crew spent an uneventful trip over the North Sea, arriving back over Beccles at around 0730 hours. By now they were in high spirits with the realisation that peace had returned, and Victor suggested to Ray Fewkes, the pilot, that they ought to "beat the town up a little bit", to wake people up and celebrate the day. The town was duly "beat up" at around 500', during which Victor decided that he would add his own gesture suitable for the occasion and loose off a Very light. What he didn't take into account, however, was that the normal height for firing such a flare was much greater, and by the time he had loaded up the pistol and was in a position to fire, the Barracuda was flying just above the rooftops. The pistol was fired, and the flare dropped out of sight, after which the crew landed at RAF Beccles. After taxying back to dispersal and switching off, the sound of fire engine bells could be clearly heard coming from the direction of the town. A couple of hours later 810's CO, Lieutenant Commander Heath, strode into the crew room and took Ray Fewkes and Victor Lease to one side. The RAF Station Commander had received a complaint from the railway station master that "some fool in an aircraft" had let off a flare which had hit the wooden part of the station roof and set it on fire. It was suggested by the CO that the crew concerned might wish to spend the day "keeping their heads down", a suggestion which they were only too glad to comply with.

The Warwick crews of 280 Sqn had already enjoyed their first peacetime flights the previous day, when a mad scramble to see who could be first into the air ensued following the radio announcement. The 9th May was to be spent celebrating on the ground, with a four course luncheon, followed by dancing at a "Grand Masquerade Ball" in the evening. In the town, the Fleet Air Arm made an impression on the locals, who were enjoying the Salvation Army playing in the centre, by arriving trouser-less on motor cycles, which had the effect of quickly dispersing the shocked band.

The following days for 810 were spent patrolling to ensure no rogue submarine commanders were ignoring the surrender, and overflying German coastal territory and occupied Europe to inspect the scars left by war. Sub Lieutenant Wright, piloting Barracuda 'Q' decided to signal the end of one patrol by "beating up" the Hague. Descending to rooftop level, the crew were amazed to see the whole town apparently on the streets, all wearing some orange clothing or accessories. The waving throng only encouraged John Wright further and, throwing the Barracuda on one wingtip, flew down the main street. Victor Lease, flying with his new pilot, suddenly noticed that the street was festooned with overhead power cables for the trams which ran there, and quickly informed John Wright, who pulled the aircraft up to a safe height before any harm was done.

On 12th May, Victor had another close call when flying with pilot Sub Lieutenant Bob Liddell in Barracuda 'H' during a formation practice. Pulling suddenly out of formation, oil streaks were seen on the canopy blisters, necessitating an immediate emergency landing to avoid the engine seizing and an even quicker descent to "Mother Earth". Fortunately for the crew, the USAAF airfield at Leiston was dead ahead, and Victor was asked to get off a red Very flare to signal that the aircraft would be coming straight into land without the usual formality of flying a circuit first. Landing safely, the American flyers gathered round the strange looking machine, by now steaming well from an overheated engine. A USAAF Captain looking on was heard to ask "Christ Almighty, does that thing really fly?" Waiting for transport back to Beccles, the crew were taken to what the Americans knew as "Chow", where they were treated to such novelties as iced coffee, followed by a visit to the Mess, where spirits appeared in innumerable supply. This was quite a shock for the Fleet Air Arm crew who, back in the RAF Beccles Mess, were used to seeing a single bottle of gin go up in the bar being emptied in 10 minutes, thereafter being forced to drink beer. Warming to the American's hospitality, the crew quite forgot about going back to Beccles until quite late, when they decided to look for the, as yet, unannounced arrival of their transport. It transpired that the driver had arrived some time earlier, and received the same level of hospitality over in the equivalent of the Airmen's Mess. This left the driver in no fit state to drive, so Bob Liddell, deemed to be the least inebriated of them all, took the wheel. Arriving back, they reported to the CO, who took one look at them, and told them to report back in the morning as he obviously wouldn't get any sense out of them, the state they were in. The diversion landing prompted a good deal of camaraderie with the Americans, who came over to RAF Beccles for a party, followed by a return visit to Leiston later. The night after the party at Beccles, a number of Mustangs beat up the airfield, much to the amusement of the Fleet Air Arm personnel and much to the annoyance of the RAF Station Commander.

On the ground, celebrations in the town included a VE Day Parade on 13th May, with 170 personnel from the airfield participating. Meanwhile, 280 Squadron played their part in the VE celebrations, dropping a lifeboat close inshore off Lowestoft as part of the nearby town's event. At the end of the month, training and navigation exercises saw the Warwicks flying all over the UK, which often included the important objective of collecting as much food and drink as possible for the regular parties in the Mess. One trip to Nutt's Corner in Northern Ireland saw a Warwick's bomb bay filled with Guinness barrels, while elsewhere on the aircraft Irish whiskey, gin and beer were stowed. Shortly after VE day, the Air Officer Commanding 16 Group visited RAF Beccles, telling the RAF personnel that they would be winding down to peacetime routine, while thanking 810 Sqn for their contribution to the effort against the mini submarines and indicating that the Fleet Air Arm element would probably be posted to the Far East, where the war against Japan was still being waged.

During the month, the ageing Walruses of 278 Sqn were supplemented by newer Supermarine Sea Otter IIs. Intended to replace the Walrus, Sea Otters didn't enter service until November 1943. Very similar looking to it's forebear, the main difference between the two types was a slightly more powerful tractor engine in the Sea Otter in place of the pusher engine of the Walrus, better range, aerodynamic and hydrodynamic performance. These characteristics combined to give greater loads, particularly important when recovering downed aircrew from the sea, and another reason for the Walruses inability to lift off following some rescues. The Sea Otter was the last biplane type to emerge from the Supermarine stable, and the only biplane to enter squadron service in the RAF during World War II. Those Sea Otters based at Beccles were the last to be operated by the RAF.

A brief visiting unit to RAF Beccles during May was 288 Anti-Aircraft Co-operation Squadron, and though the station log fails to note any dates or details of the detachment, it is known that target-towing Supermarine Spitfires were there for a short period. The unit re-equipped with the American made Vultee Vengance in May, though there is no record of these being based at RAF Beccles either.

The month of June began with a much reduced routine, the 280 Sqn aircrew having but an hour of work per day and weekends off, pending the implementation of a peacetime regime. In the meantime, each officer was allocated an extra duty or responsibility, to relieve boredom and to prepare them for their future roles. Gus Platts found himself as "Station Artist", which meant he had to make up the posters for the stations dances, and later on the role was extended to cover the whole of the Group. Another part of the role was to teach art to the airmen, and a third element was "Station Librarian". A small office was allocated for this use, which was more than ample for the single tea chest of books provided by the RAF.

To supplement the library, Gus canvassed the residents of Grove Road, where he had lodgings with his wife, Vera. The response was overwhelming, and soon the library was stacked out, sorted and marked. The first customer was the CO of 280 Sqn, followed rapidly by most of the rest of the camp. A clerk was employed to check the books in and out, for which he was paid the princely sum of 5 shillings a week. The "salary" was

The Supermarine Sea Otter's of 278 Sqn were some of the last to go into service with the RAF. Here a Fleet Air Arm example shows it's lineage from the earlier Walrus, a type it was intended to replace.
(Imperial War Museum, Neg No.MH5249)

not so much for his library duties as his role as lookout for the illicit print room adjoining the library, where Gus had an "operation" supplying posters and advertising to the town's businesses. If anyone important entered the library, his job was to come smartly to attention, stamping his foot on the floor in the process, and yelling "Sir", to signal the private posters to be hidden away and replaced with official RAF ones.

Mid afternoon on June 3rd, 810 Sqn departed from Beccles, forming up in close formation and flying low down the runway before setting course for the Royal Naval Air Station at Machrihanish, near Cambletown in Scotland. Here they were due to embark on the escort carrier HMS Queen for the Far East.

The Warwicks of 280 Sqn were called upon to cover the visit of King George VI and the Queen to the Channel Islands on 6th June, with 'X' and 'Y' positioned to RAF Northolt, near London, and 'E' to RAF Thorney Island, near Portsmouth. The following day Andy Padbury, now flying with Australian pilot Flying Officer Johnny Maxwell on this detachment, decided to fly over the Normandy invasion beaches and battlefields, followed by a sea level inspection of Brighton and Hastings piers. Later in the month, 280 became involved with the 8th US Army Air Force once more, six aircraft being despatched to the Azores to cover the heavy bombers returning to the States. This was a major logistical operation which lasted three months and sadly, despite all the efforts of the Air Sea

Rescue services, some American aircrew survived many perilous missions over Germany only to be lost on the flights home.

Back at Beccles, the arrival of 15 Air Crew Holding Unit of the Royal Australian Air Force on 17th June boosted the numbers on the station by over a thousand, pending their repatriation.

During the next couple of months training flights were the order of the day at Beccles, with the opportunity of offering flights for ground crew and Air Training Corps Cadets. Gus Platts remembered one incident that nearly brought that particular activity to a close. Women performed a variety of roles on the station from parachute packers, drivers, and mechanics to nurses and radio operators, making up a quarter of the station personnel. They mixed in with the male airmen, sharing the same deprivations, so the CO of 280 decided that, as a treat, they would all get to fly before they were de-mobbed. Tommy Pike's crew would take up the first batch of six, using the CO's own aircraft. Taking off with the girls crowded at every window, they flew lazy, wide circles for half an hour before returning to Beccles. Lowering the undercarriage for landing, one of the wheels wouldn't lock into position. The gear was retracted and then lowered again, then again after some violent manoeuvres, but with the same result. Tommy Pike took the aircraft down low over the control tower, where the operations staff scrutinised the limp leg. They continued circling the airfield to burn off fuel and weigh up the options, which were to get the girls to bail out, try a belly landing, or attempt to land tail first, gently nursing the main wheels onto the runway. None of the crew would bail out, nor would the girls, so the last option was chosen. Packing the WAAFs on the floor against a bulkhead, and bracing the area with everything they could find, the Warwick was brought in for a textbook landing, the main wheels locking forward on touchdown. The crew breathed a sigh of relief, and the CO was ecstatic that neither his precious aeroplane nor the WAAFs were damaged. However, the incident precipitated a change of heart and henceforth flights for the girls were banned for their own safety.

Local Air Cadet David Woodward logged two flights of around 15 minutes each in a biplane De Havilland Dominie communications transport from Beccles. Two crude extra seats, which resembled sawn off deckchairs, were added for the Air Experience flights.

On 3rd September, a detachment arrived from RAF Thornaby in Yorkshire, consisting of two Sea Otters and three Warwicks belonging to 279 Sqn RAF. The Squadron, whose motto was "To be and be seen", had been formed in 1941 at RAF Bircham Newton, Norfolk, for Air Sea Rescue duties, and had been the first to use airborne lifeboats.

The winding down of operations in East Anglia gave the opportunity for visits to Europe of a more friendly nature than hitherto, and Warwicks from Beccles provided Air Sea Rescue cover for American aircraft participating in an airshow at Copenhagen on 9th September. The following day, RAF

Consolidated Liberators 'N', 'P' and 'V' from 224 Sqn visited Beccles, to be joined by eleven Bristol Beaufighters of 254 Sqn and thirteen De Havilland Mosquitoes of 248 Sqn the same day. The latter unit held a tenuous connection with RAF Beccles, insofar as a detachment of five crews from 618 Sqn had been attached to 248 Sqn at Predannack during October 1943, to test the concept of using a Mosquito-mounted six pounder gun against shipping. The Liberators left the same day and the twin engined visitors two days later, when they moved to North Weald, prior to taking part in the Battle of Britain flypast over London on the 15th of the month.

October saw operations draw to a close, with 278 Sqn departing for Thorney Island over the period 18th-20th, and 280 Sqn to Langham, Norfolk on 30th. The next day, the two Sea Otters of 279 Sqn left for Wroughton, while their Warwicks joined 280's at Langham. By now, the aircrew from Canada, South Africa, Australia and New Zealand had returned home, each departure suitably marked by a boozy party. The station strength at the end of the month was 945 RAF, 182 WAAF and 430 RAAF personnel. Although the squadrons had all gone, many of their aircraft remained, mostly due to unserviceability problems. An Avro Anson communications aircraft and three Warwicks left on 1st November, again to Langham, followed by three more on 3rd and yet another three on 13th, the last for Shawbury in Wiltshire. Meanwhile, the Australian holding unit was closed down on 6th, the servicing echelon and remainder of 280 Sqn moving out the same day.

By 30th November, RAF Beccles was officially declared non-operational, leaving only a small number of personnel remaining to keep the airfield in a care and maintenance state under the control of Langham while the Air Ministry decided on it's future. The small base hospital turned over it's medical supplies, including penicillin, to the local hospital. For a while, the accommodation was used by the Royal Navy as a temporary lodging area for training reservists at RNAS Culham, Oxfordshire, known as HMS Hornbill. In this regard, Beccles was, for a short while, designated HMS Hornbill II.

CHAPTER 8

ENDINGS AND BEGINNINGS

December 1945 Onwards

The small station complement carried on their duties over the winter months, with the station Christmas party having to receive a large injection from the local populace to boost the numbers. One Warwick, serial number BV410, remained forlornly in a hangar at Beccles over the winter, due to some damage it had received during the final months of operations. David Hasprey, a Wireless Operator/Air Gunner who had moved to Thornaby with 280 Sqn after a brief stay at Langham, was part of Pilot Officer Williamson's crew detailed to collect the aircraft. The disposal of 280's aircraft was well under way by the summer of 1946, prior to the squadron's disbandment. The three crew were flown down to Beccles in an Anson, where the Warwick was handed over by the small engineering party left behind to repair the aircraft. After fuelling from a bowser which then disappeared, the crew were dismayed to find that the Warwick was reluctant to leave the ground on take off due to trouble with one of the engines. The take off was aborted and, arriving back at dispersal, the pilot refused to attempt another take off until he was satisfied the problem was solved. Two days later, on 12th July, Warwick BV410 finally left RAF Beccles. After engine test runs, there was very little fuel left in the tanks, so a stop was made at RAF North Creake to top up before moving on to Thornaby, ending the last official RAF movement in or out of Beccles.

A Prisoner of War camp was set up during 1946, and up to a thousand German prisoners were held there until 1947. Some of the accommodation was used by local people for a time, and the hangars were put to use for storage by the Ministry of Food. Even in 1946, RAF Beccles was being considered as a future base for two strike squadrons under 19 Group, but this idea was dropped with the rapid contraction of the RAF and the surfeit of East Anglian airfields with far superior accommodation and facilities. In the civil role, the 1950's saw the airfield being considered for use as an airport in support of Great Yarmouth and Lowestoft Corporations, and later as a base for flying fresh fish around the country. A new road linking Worlingham and Hulver put paid to all these ideas, as it cut through all the runways and effectively made further use by large aircraft impossible. It was around this time that two more aircraft made emergency landings on the airfield. Firstly, in 1950, a Gloster Meteor F Mk 8 jet fighter lost a canopy in flight, requiring a replacement to be flown in from RAF Horsham St Faith (now Norwich Airport) via an Avro Anson. Before it arrived, an overnight stay in one of the hangars, with the nose and engine nacelles outside of the doors, required a guard from the Horsham St Faith crash crew. Two airmen, dressed in green rubber kerosene suits, were assigned to the task. During the evening, it started to rain, and so the airman climbed into the engine nacelles for shelter, while discharging their duty to stay on guard. Some time later, three boys appeared on cycles and, laying them down to approach on foot, were allowed to get quite close to the aircraft before the two airmen jumped out, causing the boys to flee in panic! Later, a twin-boom tail De Havilland Vampire jet fighter sought refuge on a Beccles runway after running low on fuel. A local man cycling across the airfield got a rude shock when he found himself pursued by a much faster "three wheeler" whistling along close behind. The hot efflux from the aircraft's jet pipe set fire to the grass round part of the perimeter track.

A sign of the only long term aviation related future for the airfield came in the 1950s, when a Sikorsky S-51 of British European Airways (BEA) Helicopter Experimental Unit visited briefly on a pioneering Royal Mail service. With the discovery of the natural gas fields in the Southern North Sea in 1965, helicopter operators began moving into the area in support of drilling, construction and eventually production operations. Among them was BEA Helicopters Limited. This became British Airways Helicopters in 1974, and then British International Helicopters from 1986, after Robert Maxwell's Mirror Group of companies took over. Operating up to four Sikorsky S-61Ns, primarily for Shell Exploration and Production, the early contracts attracted business for the main runway in the form of visiting fixed-wing aircraft of Shell Aviation, among the larger being a four engine De Havilland Heron. Later, other helicopter varieties were introduced, including Sikorsky S-58Ts, Bell 212s, Westland WG30s and Sikorsky S-76s. With the gradual deterioration of the main runway, it's use was finally curtailed following a minor landing accident with a light aircraft, but a section of the northernmost taxiway was still used in the early 1970's by crop-sprayers, including Piper Pawnees of Westwick Aviation. Visiting aircraft overflying the site included, in the 1970's, a flying display rehearsal of an experimental Sikorsky S-67 Blackhawk attack helicopter, together with a large Sikorsky S-65 Sea Stallion, preparing for display at Farnborough. The weekend following the Blackhawk, attempting a loop, crashed onto Farnborough airfield in an inverted position, tragically killing the pilot.

Due to changes in take-off procedures and the need for a light aircraft strip, British International Helicopters opened up the 500 metre section of the main runway adjacent to their facilities on the eastern side of the airfield as far as the B1127 road. This was linked by a taxiway to the loop dispersals and T2 hangar, forming a large area of the heliport. Several very popular open days were held over the years, and visiting light aircraft combined with the resident helicopters to provide a small air display. A little known facet of the BIH operation was a paint spray facility for military helicopters, which was shrouded in secrecy for security reasons, but which resulted in

British Airways Sikorsky S-61N lands at Ellough Heliport after a flight to Shell's Southern North Sea gas fields. The S-61N carried 19 passengers, and was, for many years, the workhorse of the base's fleet (author).

new fencing being erected to deter prying eyes.

Sadly, the excellent offshore support operation at Beccles came to an abrupt end in the mid-1990's, when Shell awarded their contract to KLM-ERA at Norwich, using Sikorsky S-76B's. With their major client in the Southern North Sea gone, British International Helicopters had little choice but to close their base, making a dedicated team redundant and resulting in a lot of peripheral business being lost to the local area.

In 1996, a new company took over the BIH site, operating fixed wing services in the form of aircraft training, maintenance and accident repair facilities. To promote the flying training side of the business, the Chief Instructor flew a Cessna 150 Aerobat the short hop from the airstrip onto the main section of the old runway, in order to promote the business at the Sunday Market! Beccles Aviation Limited had moved from nearby Seething, but were unfortunately unable to lease the hangars they had left behind, and took the difficult commercial decision to move back to Seething shortly afterwards. In 1997, the current incumbent of the remaining usable section of the main runway, Rainair, gained a licence to operate from the CAA, and has steadily built up the facilities to include a small hangar, clubhouse, and training facilities.

A rare British Airways Westland WG30 taxying along the loop dispersal adjacent to the easternmost T2 hangar. The WG30 was developed from the military Lynx helicopter, but did not enjoy the same success. An example was, however, sent to Agusta in Italy, and formed the basis of the successful Agusta Westland AW139 medium helicopter (author).

Cessna 150's and a Cessna 175 operate from the part concrete, part grass, 800 metre strip, together with microlights and light helicopters. The only licenced airfield in Suffolk, the business held events attracting the likes of the Royal Aero Club, who held an international precision flying championship there in September 2003. A further dimension to the airborne activities arrived in January 2010, with the transfer of UK Parachuting's training school from Old Buckenham, Norfolk. The sight and sounds of a Cessna Caravan and the opening of parachutes is now a regular feature above the airfield and it's surroundings.

The development of an industrial estate has encroached further onto the taxiways and runways, although the setting up of a Sunday Market along the main runway has led to some resurfacing and a general improvement to the degradations in the surface. Over the years, many local and national businesses have set up on the site, bringing employment and opportunities for nearby businesses and residents. Many of the original buildings remain, mostly serving as industrial units. The westernmost T2 hangar is used for storage by Polimoon, who have a large plastic container factory on the boundary of the old airfield. A new link road to the A146 was built in 1990, partially along the path of the old North/South runway. The old control tower stood in a copse in the centre of the airfield, derelict beside the overgrown slit trenches that offered shelter from enemy attacks which never materialised. It was finally demolished in around 2009.

Although the gradual transformation from airfield to industrial estate is under way, compared to many, more prestigious and famous wartime airfields, RAF Beccles, or Ellough as most local people know it, remains substantially intact. There are plans to name some of the roads on the industrial park after aircraft which have operated from the airfield, and already an Anson Way has appeared off the link road to the A146. Unlike many wartime airfields in the UK, aviation activity has remained an important and visible link to it's heritage. Long may the link, and the airfield, continue.

Pictured in 2009, the main runway is broken into two sections, the nearest used by the Sunday Market, the further, narrower one by Rainair. The outline of Ellough Raceway kart circuit and the industrial development, can be clearly seen (Bob Ward).

Editor's Notes

1) The emergency landing of B-17F Flying Fortress "Herky Jerky II" on 10th October 1943 is featured in the original print of this book. In one aviation publication, it is reported to have taken place at RAF Beccles. I have since discovered that the official history of the 95th Bomb Group states that it occurred at Thorpe Abbotts, near Scole, Suffolk. I have therefore taken the opportunity to remove reference to this particular incident in the reprint.

2) In the process of my research, I have come across several books referring to 279 Squadron remaining at RAF Beccles until March 1946, and re-equipping with Avro Lancaster ASR Mk IIIs during their stay. Whilst I acknowledge the Lancaster link to 279 Sqn, I have found no evidence to suggest that Lancasters were ever based at RAF Beccles. Eyewitnesses at the time, including aircrew who had flown the type from other airfields, categorically insist that Lancasters were never at Beccles. It is conceivable that the occasional aircraft may have visited on a navigational exercise, either overflying or carrying out the odd landing, but anything more is unsubstantiated, according to my research.